What people are saying about

How to win when dealing with builders

This book teaches the simple secrets of success when dealing with builders. It is filled with fun-packed, real-life stories that will amuse and educate you. It's full of practical information in "layman's language" on how to negotiate and protect yourself from possibly painful situations. If you're serious about saving yourself time and money, you've got to read this book.

Robert G. Allen, bestselling author of the New York Times', *Nothing Down*, *Creating Wealth*, and *Multiple Streams of Income*.

Reading '**How to win when dealing with builders**' really gave me invaluable knowledge. Being a single parent means I am having to take the word of people and companies I don't know when I am wanting work done within my home. I have the knowledge and confidence to ask them questions and understand what the answers should be. This has also made sure I am not fleeced by any would-be conman. Even the smallest of things, such as when I prepared my son's bedroom to be decorated, I went out and bought everything I needed – using correct terminology, buying things I needed as opposed to things that I don't really need. A really enjoyable read, I loved picturing the examples given and the antics of Bruiser Bruce and the Author. It made me want to continue reading as I feel I gained a great

3

amount of knowledge along with laughter and humour. A fantastic insight into what could happen if you don't do your homework.

Tracey Morewood, West Yorkshire

LaVern Brown successfully shares his 40 years' experience in the building trade, helping the reader become more confident with building terms and dealing with builders. His blend of real life stories and factual accounts engages the reader throughout, while his characters are both horrifying and humorous. Not only will you take away lessons in how to win when dealing with builders, you will also feel uplifted by the life lessons included along the way.

Kelly Nicholls, Derbyshire

How to win when dealing with builders

"If you're serious about saving yourself time and
money, you've got to read this book"

Robert G. Allen, *New York Times* bestselling author

LaVern Brown

Published by
nabbab

www.nabbab.com

How to win when dealing with builders

Published by nabbab

Contact information for request for permission to reproduce or distribute materials available through this book is listed below.

Website: www.nabbab.com

Email: info@nabbab.com

ISBN: 978-0-9571403-0-1

6

Acknowledgements

It's so easy to forget all of those people who have had a part in producing this book, even though they may never know. I could never have imagined when I first started out in the building industry that I would, at some stage in my life, actually sit down and write a book.

I'd like to thank my mother for all she did for me and the values she instilled in me as I was growing from a boy to a man. I still feel her influence in my life at times and the values she helped me adhere to when I have to make important decisions.

Thank you to New York Times bestselling author Robert G. Allen for his kind words in endorsing this book, and for his time and effort in supporting and freely giving of his knowledge, not only to me but to people all over the world.

Reading has been a love of my life as far back as I can remember. Someone once said to me that 'Knowledge is powerful' and I've always believed this to be true. As the years have passed by and I've been able to be part of the education system, I've found that this is only partly true. I've learnt that knowledge is powerful when you know what to do with it.

I'd like to thank my mentor as I started out in the building industry; a man I shall always remember and be grateful to, Derek Day. Derek was a bricklayer who

7

taught me all he knew and more. He taught me how to use the knowledge he gave me, not only to be able to build structures but to help build people. Derek was a master builder in so many ways.

More recently, a thank you to people I've come to know and again been influenced by due to their willingness to give of their services without asking for something in return. To Tracey for the time and help she has freely given me, for allowing me to call and ask for advice and guidance, and for helping me with my computer needs. Thank you to Kelly for sorting out the proof reading and editing for me.

The list could go on and on; there are so many people who have influenced me in writing this book. I'd just like to thank you, the general public, property investors, and builders, for purchasing and reading this book, because it was written for you. I hope that you will enjoy what you read and apply the knowledge that has been given. Thank you.

My Special Thank You

I would like to give a special thank you to my One in a Trillion wife, Anne-Katrine.

My Eternal companion and my best friend, whose love and support I can never thank her enough for.

To the person who has been there for me when I was searching for my meaning in life.

I thank her for allowing me to be able to search in my own world, for what I needed to do.

I thank her for the special person she is and for having faith in me when I doubted myself.

I hope that one day I will be worthy enough to be with her throughout Eternity.

Thank you my Anne-Ki.

How to win when dealing with builders

Table of Contents

11

12

Introduction

The reason for writing this book, **How to win when dealing with builders**, was due to people continually asking, "How do I win when dealing with builders?" They wanted to ask someone who was experienced, who would give an honest answer, someone they could trust. They wanted to be told how things are without the bull. They said that they couldn't find a source for the information they wanted anywhere and we were recommended by people who knew us. Locally, me and Bruiser Bruce have become the Marjorie Proops[1] of our profession, it seems.

To be honest, it got to the point where it was cheesing me off, being asked the same question over and over again, **How to win when dealing with builders**. So, I thought I would have a word with my mate Bruiser Bruce to see if we could put an end to it. Bruiser suggested I let him have a word, if people keep pestering me. Bruiser is very protective of me, you see. But, being the gentleman that I am, I thought there might be a better way of helping people: sharing mine and Bruiser's considerable knowledge in writing this book.

When we thought about how we could help the ordinary Joe Bloggs in relation to our experiences, it was a no brainer really. Me and Bruiser put our heads together and decided, I do the writing and he gives his input through me. It's a genius of an idea, even if I do

---

1 Marjorie Proops was an agony aunt best known for her column in the Daily Mirror.

13

say so myself. You see, I used to come second in English at school; it was my favourite subject. (A classmate named Ian Wright always used to come first. It drove me crazy!) So, this is my first experience of becoming another Bill Shakespeare. Hey, you never know.

You see, I am the brains and Bruiser is the brawn of our building work partnership. We have been together for over 40 years, and it doesn't seem a day too long. Anyway, you're going to get our knowledge on **How to win when dealing with builders**, who are part of our beloved industry. The deal is this; me and Bruiser shall be answering questions I have been given by punters from all walks of life. We are going to say it the way it is, in our opinion, and leave it for you to decide if it makes sense. At the end of the day, it will be down to you to decide.

Think like a wise man but communicate in the language of the people. **William Butler Yeats**

You shall be hearing it from me and Bruiser, by us telling you about our work experiences and how we dealt with things. At times, I shall be questioning Bruiser and you shall be seeing things from our point of view as builders. We shall be giving you our opinion on what we think you, as punters, should do to protect yourselves as well. The good thing is you don't have to do anything you don't want to do, but we don't want you to get **ripped off**: it can be very painful. People who have tried to rip me and Bruiser off can testify to that. If you're looking for someone who can write well, has great spelling, dots the is and cross the ts in the

14

right places, you may need to look elsewhere. As long as you can understand what me and Bruiser are saying and it makes sense, what more do you want? This is causing us a right headache, writing this book, but we believe we need to give back. It's hard work but we're used to that.

Me and Bruiser have done all right out of our game and want to put the **credibility** back into the building industry. We are hoping that this book will be the start for us to be able to help you in many more areas, when we get your feedback. We will share with you our life experiences, which have made us rich in knowledge, and our advice and guidance if you want it. This is what this book is all about, **helping you**!

Why? Because we care about people and don't want you to get ripped off (like loads of other people), because you don't know any better. We don't have all the answers, but if we don't know, we'll know a man who does. So, have a read and we can go from there. Fair enough?

About The Authors

My creds

My name is LaVern Brown and I use my initials LB, mainly so my cred will not go right out of the window. How can a builder have a name like mine, I've been thinking to myself. It doesn't give me much credibility. I bet you are thinking the same. My name sounds more like a Tamla Motown or film star (I wish, by the way). I have been called worse, mind. Well, first, let's get one thing straight. I wasn't brought up with a silver spoon in my mouth. (Come to think about it, when Sunday came around, my mum did get the silver plated spoons out for tea, but you know what I'm saying).

Don't get me wrong, me and my twin sister never went hungry, but it wasn't easy back in the so-called good old days. My mum worked hard bringing us up: she was a boot and shoe machinist. My hometown is a place called Northampton; it's around 70 miles north of London. In those days, it was known for the boot and shoe industry. Our local football team, Northampton Town FC, are nicknamed The Cobblers (cobblers being shoe repairers). When you see them play, you know why their nickname is The Cobblers (sorry, lads!)

They used to call me Sponge Head when I was at school, due to the afro. For a laugh, when it was raining, my hair seemed to soak up the water, and I used to shower people by pulling my head back as far as I could and moving it forward at speed to soak them. The amount of water that used to come out was amaz-

16

ing. So, that's how Sponge Head came about. (It brings back some great memories).

Anyway, when I left school I didn't stay on because there was plenty of work about in those days. To be honest, I bet they were glad to see the back of me and Bruiser; we got up to no end of mischief, but that's for another book. So, off I went into the big bad world to get into the building game as an apprentice bricklayer. (Apprentice is what the term **time-served** is referring to in this book).

Over 40 years later, you name it, I've probably done it. New build houses, industrial units, stonework, refurbishment work. I've been a college lecturer (I bet that surprised you), I've taught in a prison (that's probably not surprised you), and no, it wasn't at Her Majesty's Pleasure. I also became an NVQ Assessor. Even though I say it myself, I'm no muppet! Mind you, it would be to my benefit for you to believe that I'm a muppet, when I'm around your house giving you some spiel on what you want doing workwise. You shall see where I'm coming from with this statement, further on in the book.

By the way, I have a Master's degree in NTAC (Not Taking Any Crud): I'm too old and good-looking for all of that. I was going to say ugly, but that's my partner Bruiser's features.

Oh, and I drive a V registration Vauxhall Astra. Why? Because I want to! Look, I can go out and buy a Jag or something similar, but, at the moment, I don't want one. I know what I'm worth and that's all that matters to me. Me and Bruiser deal with millionaires all of the time, we associate with them, spend time with them. Don't be fooled by what you see at times when dealing with people, because you never know. What's that old saying? "Never judge a book by its cover." Hey, let that be a warning to you for future reference.

Bruiser's creds

What can I say about my mate Bruiser Bruce other than he's one in a billion. I suppose, when it comes down to it, I can honestly say that I love him!

Don't get me wrong, I'm not gay, (that used to mean happy in my day, actually) so let's not go down that path. Look, people are people wherever you go, some good and some bad. But my mate Bruiser is different, if that makes sense. He's got a heart of gold and wouldn't hurt a fly, but don't upset him!

Let me try to describe Bruiser. He's 6 foot 3 and looks like he's done 10 rounds with Mike Tyson. He wears size 15 boots; he has the build of a silver back gorilla (come to think about it, he even walks like one). He's as strong as an ox and has the mind-set of Baloo the bear. Oh, and he's scared of spiders. But you still wouldn't want to get on the wrong side of him.

Me and Bruiser go back to our school days where he seemed to latch on to me, and at times he made me cry with laughter. Whenever we got the cane or slipper in those days, he was always the first to have it. To be honest, I conned him into going first, so that when it

18

was my turn, just the thought of seeing how Bruiser responded made me laugh so much it didn't really hurt me. There were occasions when Bruiser took my punishment for me. Why you might ask? I guess because he loved me too. Blimey, I'll be filling up soon.

As I was saying, Bruiser is as strong as an ox and is a man of few words. Actually, come to think about it, it's probably because he's not very good at reading. Besides, he doesn't have to say much: you can tell when he's got the hump or when he's in a good mood, so you just let him do his own thing. Bruiser may not be good at reading but he is good with figures. Yes, he may do a lot of counting on his fingers, but don't be fooled by that.

He is a shrewd businessman, our Bruiser, and is worth a lot of money, a bit like myself: worth a lot, but doesn't have a lot!

Bruiser started as a hod carrier and then progressed to becoming a bricklayer; he used to say before he became a bricklayer, that I was a glorified hod carrier. He might be right, but back in those days good hod carriers were worth their weight in gold, in my opinion. It was hard work, up and down ladders all day with bricks, blocks, and mortar. I was bright enough not to do all that hard work.

Hard work never killed anyone, so why take a chance? **Unknown**

Like I said, I'm the brains and Bruiser is the brawn (but

19

that's digressing.) Actually, I shall continue to digress most of the time, so that you shall hopefully get the points me and Bruiser want you to remember. Again, it's so that you can visualise through our stories the points we want you to remember. Apparently, pictures are a great way for us humans to remember things.

If you remember the stories that's where the protection is. Get it? Trust me on this, it's very clever stuff. Bruiser has done all of the same work I've done and definitely has the same Master's degree in **NTAC** (remember what it stands for?) The only difference is your feet may not touch the ground if Bruiser feels he is being given **crud**.

Thank you for bearing with me on my description of me and Bruiser. Because we are real people, it's been very important to get a picture of us and our characters within your mind. Unfortunately (or fortunately, depending on how you look at it), there are thousands of me and Bruisers out there. We are the good blokes though, who are here to try to help and advise you in making the right choices and decisions when you are learning **How to win when dealing with builders**.

SECTION 1:
What do you really want?

Look, during me and Bruiser's journey in the building game, if we had a pound for all the times people didn't really know what they were looking for, we would be even wealthier by now. (As I said, old Bruiser is worth a bob or two, but he will never admit it).

Think about it, **what do you really want**? Ultimately, everything we do in our life is driven by our fundamental **need to avoid pain** and our desire to **gain pleasure**.

How many times have you heard about someone who had won the lottery, only to find that when they got the money they were looking for, it didn't bring them happiness.

Why?

Because they didn't know what to do with the money when they got it. Nobody had taught them how to deal with money, so having money didn't bring them the happiness money could bring.

Make sense? My mate Tony says it better:

Anything you think you want, you only want because of the feeling you think obtaining it will give you. **Anthony Robbins**

"Bruiser, do you remember the extension we built for Mr Decisive, (our nickname for him) who decided after it was built that it wasn't what he really wanted?"

"Yeah, he was a dickhead!" I told you Bruiser was a man of few words.

By the way, there may be some words you come across that you are not familiar with, so at the back of this book you will find their meaning. It just saves me having to go over everything again. Besides, it saves me from feeling like I'm your mum, having to explain everything to you. Mind you, I have been called worse in my time, like I've said.

On this occasion, I shall explain what Bruiser is actually saying though, when calling Mr Decisive a dickhead. What Bruiser is saying is that Mr Decisive was stupid. Actually, Bruiser said a little more, but just in case it's before 9 o'clock at night when you're reading this, I shall keep it to myself. Harsh words, but it's because he cares.

This was a job we were given by a contractor. We were given a drawing by the contractor that showed a single storey brick and block extension onto the back of Mr Decisive's house. Apparently, after speaking to Mr Decisive once the job was completed, he told us he knew the contractor well and didn't want to offend him. This had nothing to do with Mr Decisive having any fear of the contractor; it was due to him liking him, as I can remember.

So, what was the problem you might ask?

Mr Decisive said to us, and I quote, "I didn't really want this!"

Apparently, what he really wanted was a dwarf brick and block work wall built, so that he could have a UPVC conservatory structure on top.

Unbelievable, you might say. But I can tell you similar stories that would make your hair curl, come to think about it, your toes too.

There is a wise old saying:

"You've got to be careful what you ask for, because you might get it!"

Admittedly, this is an extreme example, but it is a true example of how some people think, and what people do.

I couldn't get my head around how Mr Decisive actually saw the drawings prior to me and Bruiser starting the work and still didn't say anything to the contractor. We only found out what his problem was because we asked the question.

I'll re-phrase that. I asked Mr Decisive (Bruiser being a man of few words) why he kept looking at what we were doing, in the way that he was. If nothing else, it taught me and Bruiser another lesson of life:

24

"Always double check or treble check what a punter really wants by asking questions."

We strongly recommend that you, as punters, make it very clear what you want as well.

How? By having **what you really want written down** on paper. It's called a **contract**.

Look, at times, a contract isn't worth the paper it's written on, but it gives support if problems arise later.

Remember: To avoid pain and to gain pleasure in our game, you need to know what you really want and how to go about getting it. Actually, I am not telling you the truth; there is one thing, no, two things that are 100% true.

What are they, you might ask.
1. We are going to die. Fact!
2. Me and Bruiser always get paid. Fact!

We have learnt in this game that you may think and believe that you will get 100% perfection, but that will not be the case. Me and Bruiser can go and find fault with anything someone does; trust me. And, we know what we're looking for.

So again, to avoid pain, **don't expect perfection**. Bonus!

When I received my NEBOSH qualification in Health and Safety there were two terms that always reared

25

their ugly heads (again depending on your viewpoint): **Reasonably Practicable** and **Adequately Sufficient**.

What do these terms mean? References in the *Oxford Reference Dictionary* states:

Reasonable... *Having or based on sound judgement or moderation; sensible, not expecting too much.* (Page 689)

Practicable... *That can be done or used; possible in practice.* (Page 654)

Adequate... *Sufficient, satisfactory; passable but not outstandingly good.* (Page 7)

Sufficient... *Enough.* (Page 824)

What we are saying here is, "**If you don't expect perfection, you are not going to be disappointed when you don't get it!**"

Make sense? Be **reasonable**! We are just trying to help you to become **realistic**!

So don't try to be an expert.

Have you ever heard the expression, "**Stick to what you know and leave the rest to them that know what they are doing**?" (Or words to that affect).

Since we've had these property programmes pop up on TV, it seems there are so many people who think they are building work experts, after watching them. Don't

26

get me wrong, I'm not saying you can't learn some-thing from these programmes, but to go out into the real world and earn a living from watching them is an-other matter.

Yes, I know there are those of you who have been taught by me and Bruiser in the past, on how to build a garden wall. We've taught you the skills of how to build, and some of you have actually gone out and made some money.

I'm not talking about that.

I'm talking about going out and doing work that you know how to do; I'm talking about knowing what to do to overcome some nightmare problems that you may be faced with. This type of skill only comes through **lifetime experience and skill.**

"Ignorance is bliss until it catches up with you!"

Just something to think about…

Summary
- **Mr Decisive**
- **Be careful what you ask for**
- **Don't expect perfection**
- **Don't try to be an expert**
- **Lifetime experience and skill**

How to win when dealing with builders

SECTION 2:
Gypsy Jim and Doctor Doolittle

Actually, let's ask Bruiser a question in relation to this story first.

"Bruiser, do you remember the job we went to when Doctor Doolittle started to give us some verbal about what he expected us to do? Do you remember? We were expected to take over the job that some other builder had walked away from after they had started it?"

"Yeah! He was another dickhead!"

I thought I wouldn't get much from Bruiser today; I must have caught him on one of his good days. He can be hard work!

Before we move on with the story, I think it would be a good opportunity to give you some further background info in relation to Bruiser's generally limited vocabulary. I know I explained a little in Bruiser's cred section at the beginning, but this is to do with the words 'dickhead' and 'dick'.

You will find that Bruiser refers to some people as one or the other. I put this down to an experience many years ago that involved Bruiser and Gypsy Jim, the ground worker.

Now, Gypsy Jim was a typical ground worker in those

29

days. He used to have steak for breakfast and dinner, and had a big beer belly to hold all of that food in. His trousers came way down under his belly and the rear of his trousers always showed his **builder's crack** when he bent over. Builder's crack is the term we within the building industry use when part of a workman's buttocks are exposed, due to the size of their belly when they bend over.

Now, Gypsy Jim liked a fight, it seemed to be something he was addicted to. Unfortunately, Gypsy Jim seemed to have a problem with Bruiser for some unknown, very unwise reason. Gypsy Jim was intent on trying to make Bruiser look stupid in front of people (or, rather, more stupid than he actually looked).

He tried to make Bruiser look stupid in front of the whole work force actually, on this particular day. All joking aside, there was no need for this because Bruiser is one of the most amiable people you could ever come across.

But, like I said, don't make him angry.

Now I tried to calm Bruiser down and not allow Gypsy Jim to wind him up, but Gypsy Jim seemed intent on having his daily fight. So, there was a showdown between Bruiser and Gypsy, and it came to blows, on a warm summer's afternoon at a place called Crick. (We called Jim Gypsy, because he travelled around in a caravan from site to site).

Anyway, I tried to tell Gypsy that he would be losing

30

this one, but he wouldn't listen. You see Gypsy loved a fight and the adrenalin was no doubt rushing through his body. Well, to cut a long story short, just before an ambulance was called for Gypsy, he was able to kick poor old Bruiser in his prized assets with his size 12 monkey boot.

That's right; Gypsy kicked him right between Bruiser's legs. Now I knew Bruiser was really hurt by the look in his eyes. I must admit, you don't often see Bruiser hurt. When the cowardly kick was planted between Bruiser's legs, a loud scream of "**Geronimo**!" could be heard echoing across the site. (This came from Bruiser's mouth by the way).

Why Geronimo? Well, that's another story when Bruiser had a Vindaloo curry in an Indian restaurant. In fact, that's probably for another book (funny story though). Don't get me wrong. I know you may think I'm being a little selfish where Bruiser was concerned, but I felt as though my hands were tied. Look, me and Bruiser go back a long way, so can you imagine my dilemma seeing someone I've grown to love look at me with those big, sad eyes as if to say, "Please help the pain go away!"

To be fair to the medics who came for Gypsy, they did offer to take Bruiser to one side, to see if his prized assets were all intact, but Bruiser being Bruiser declined the offer. I think it was a man thing, he probably felt embarrassed. Look, I was a father figure to old Bruiser, and I feel ashamed to say that I didn't offer more comfort to him.

31

Bruiser is a big kid at heart and as a parent you would want to make things better, but I must admit that I bottled it. You've been in the situation when your child has hurt itself and you have either rubbed the pain away or kissed it better. Well, I realised then that I had a healthy love for Bruiser, in my opinion. I didn't feel inclined to do either.

Our relationship to this day is purely platonic, I'm happy to say. Fortunately for Bruiser, they weren't steel toecap boots that Gypsy was wearing. Actually, much more fortunate for Gypsy, come to think about it.

Now this caused a swelling of Bruiser's prized assets, which to this day I don't believe he psychologically ever got over. I remember he walked around for about 10 days as if he'd been riding a horse, which didn't make Bruiser a happy bunny. From then on, he seemed to have the words 'dick' and 'dickhead' embedded in his vocabulary. I can't for the life of me understand why.

Unfortunately, Gypsy's employment status came to an immediate end, due to him being on traction in the local general hospital. Again, I believe this caused trauma with withdrawal symptoms for Gypsy, because he never did return to resume his employment.

Well, let it be said, there is always something to be learnt. Unfortunately for Gypsy, he learnt the hard way. We don't want you to learn the hard way!

Right, let's get back to the Doctor Doolittle story. We called this doctor bloke Doctor Doolittle. Why? Be-

32

cause I think he thought he was talking to a couple of animals. (Now in relation to Bruiser's appearance, he could be mistaken for a primate species, but Doctor Doolittle was totally out of order).

We builders like a laugh (believe it or not) but what we don't like is being taken for idiots.

Now some of you may be thinking or saying, "Well most builders are idiots, in my experience!" Let me tell you something. You may be right to a degree, when referring to many people in life, but when someone is trying to prevent a possible future pain from occurring it's a wise thing for you not to get on the wrong side of those people. Not only for the physical pain you may receive, but also for the unforeseen pain you may experience. In fact, that's in relation to everyday life, come to think about it.

Does that make sense?

Me and Bruiser could see straightaway that there was a problem here with Doctor Doolittle. When we turned up, I said to Bruiser, "What do you think?" His reply was, "You know what I think, don't be a dick!"

Now, I have been called many things in my time by experts (trust me) but never a mind reader. (Good old Bruiser).

Actually, there is someone. My missus expects me to know why she is upset sometimes, even though she doesn't know herself. But, again, that's for another

33

book. But on this occasion, anyone who is experienced in our game would hear the **alarm bells** ringing in their head, or have that **gut feeling**. So I knew what Bruiser was referring to.

What was it, you may be thinking.

Well, the job was started but not finished. In fact, the job was an extension to his house and the footings had been started and then left. Make sure, if this happens to you, that you have a good reason for this happening and you can explain.

Why? Because you are wide open for **pain**!

There have been numerous times when me and Bruiser have just driven by when looking at jobs, due to the **alarm bells** ringing in our heads or that **gut feeling**. You develop a sixth sense over the years. The important thing is to give some feedback over the phone when dealing with us builders, as to what has happened before you ask us to come and give a price for the job to be done.

Doctor Doolittle made the **first mistake** in not telling us what to expect. In fact, he was lucky we actually went in to have a word with him anyway. (He may not have thought so before we left, mind). The only reason we went in was due to Bruiser wanting to stretch his legs because his prized assets were throbbing and giving him some grief. (All that sitting down because of us driving to the job, you see).

34

I said to Bruiser, for a laugh, "It could have been worse."

"How?"

I said, "It could have been me!"

Even Bruiser laughed at that one. Mind you, it's only because it's me. Don't you try it!

The **second mistake** was Doctor Doolittle tried to be funny.

It's great to be able to have a laugh with people; but doing it in a natural way is the key. But when you have something to hide, the eyes give it away every time, in my opinion.

What made it worse was when Doctor Doolittle made reference to how Bruiser was walking and said he hoped we hadn't parked our horses on his driveway (referring to us looking like a couple of cowboy builders). Well, this went down about as quickly as poor old Gypsy did a week or so earlier, and we know he was still recovering.

Doctor Doolittle had no chance.

Bruiser was not amused and told him so in no uncertain terms. (Ladies, you wouldn't want to know what he said, trust me. The look was bad enough!) His whole attitude was wrong in the way he spoke.

Comments like "Make sure you do a good job!" and

35

"You won't get paid if..." went down like the *Titanic*.

We weren't interested in working for him anyway, and if we did do some work for him it would have been a win-win situation for both parties, not all loaded one way.

Always remember that in the building game the local professionals know each other, so word gets around. Yes, you have people come from other areas to work, but that is where you have to be more careful.

Do your due diligence!

We found out that Doctor Doolittle had tried to tell our mates previously how to do their job and his being an arrogant dipstick didn't go down very well. So they picked up their tools and off they went. Simply, they didn't want the grief so they left.

Doctor Doolittle had a nightmare to get the work completed, and it cost him a small fortune to go with it.

When dealing with builders, use the **alarm bells/gut feeling** senses yourself. We all have them. If it doesn't sound or feel right, it probably isn't!

Doctor Doolittle caused himself **pain** because he went about dealing with builders in the wrong way. We builders are no different from any other people; we have flesh and bone, have feelings, emotions, and want to be loved. (It must be the female side of me coming out

36

at times). Seriously though, treat people as you want to be treated yourself and generally it will work out.

We know that some builders would have taught him a lesson by completing the job, making sure they got some money up front. Then they would have made sure he would have had problems with the work they did in the future. This is what I was referring to in the creds section when I said about you being given spiel so that you could be ripped off by me. There are ways of hiding bad workmanship if you know what you are doing. Trust me; you need to make sure you protect yourself. We shall be dealing with this subject further on in the book.

Basically, Doctor Doolittle caused himself **unnecessary pain**.

I go back to the quote I stated earlier. **"You've got to be careful what you ask for, because you might get it!"** So, **be wise**!

Summary
- **Doctor Doolittle**
- **Gypsy Jim**
- **Don't learn the hard way**
- **Listen for alarm bells**
- **Go on gut feelings**
- **Don't try to be an expert**
- **Do your due diligence**
- **Treat people with respect**
- **Be wise**

How to win when dealing with builders

SECTION 3:
What is a building contractor/ subcontractor?

Building contractor

I've been asked this question by loads of people: "What is a building contractor?" Well, it's someone who puts in a **bid** for a job and gets subcontractors to work on the job if the bid is won. The contractor can also work on the job. Me and Bruiser have been contractors even though we have been laying bricks as well. Get it? A contractor is responsible for the building contract. Me and Bruiser started off on small jobs and then progressed to bigger jobs. Small jobs are called **Residential work** (building houses) and **Commercial work** (factories, offices) is referred to as bigger jobs. Once you progress onto bigger projects, the more grief there can be, because you are dealing with more people, namely a **work force**.

The people who work for the contractor are called subcontractors (carpenters, plasterers, plumbers, etc.) and employees. So you need to know what you are doing. Make sure that when you have someone doing building work for you they have **insurance**. This insurance is usually called self-employed **public liability insurance**. It protects you and the contractor if anything goes wrong during the work project.

39

For example:

If a fire was caused that was traced back to the contractor, the funds are in place to take care of that and cover for personal injury of individuals who sustain injury by or under the direction of the insured contractor while working.

There are other terms that can be included but these cover it.

Subcontractors

Subcontractors are essentially tradesmen who are working within the building industry such as plumbers, carpenters, painters, etc. All of these tradesmen have different skills they can perform.

There are those in the building game who are known as Jack-Of-All-Trades and master of none. They are not officially qualified in any particular area, but can do many different jobs.

You find these people working in maintenance type work, or what we call jobbing building work. Again, they are skilled people without the pieces of paper to say they are qualified.

40

Summary

- **Building contractor**
  - Someone who puts in bids for work
  - Responsible for building contracts
  - Make sure they have public liability insurance
- **Subcontractor**
  - Tradesmen with different skills

How to win when dealing with builders

SECTION 4:
How to find a good tradesperson

"Bruiser, how do you find a good builder?"

"Tell them to ask Dick Tracy or Michael Miles!"

Bruiser is rolling about on the floor laughing right now; he looks like a beached Whale. This is Bruiser's sense of humour. Sorry!

Dick Tracy was a police detective cartoon character who would solve cases by relentless pursuit of the criminal.

Become a Dick Tracy. Here Bruiser is referring to becoming a detective when looking for a builder.

Where would a good detective look?

What would they be looking for?

What questions would they be asking?

We shall try to give some answers to the above questions, but when you really start looking, you may find them where you least expected (law of attraction and all that).

When you think about it, you are no different from Dick Tracy because you want the same as him. Once upon a time pubs used to be sociable establishments

43

where you could find every trade known to man. You would go down to the local pub and ask for whatever trade you are looking for. The fact is you still can. Not so many people go into pubs now, but they are still a good source to find who you are looking for.

You look on the TV and you come across programmes like *Cowboy Builders*.

Well, the cowboys are still there to be found, but there are also some good tradesmen out there too.

Police would still go looking in pubs for rogue builders, so you should go looking for the good ones in the same place. (Only if you want to, that is). I bet if you went in and asked someone if they know a good builder, you would get a contact. Check them out though. Again, do your **due diligence** and ask the questions.

A bit further on in the book, you will see what techniques me and Bruiser have used in the past, when checking out builders.

Michael Miles was a TV presenter who hosted the TV programme Take Your Pick. This programme was shown in the 70s, and contestants were offered money for the key to the box they had won. The contestants had a choice of opening the box to see what was in it or take the money offered. They knew there were good prizes and **booby prizes.**

What me and Bruiser are trying to say is that there are plenty of boxes out there where you would be able to

44

find a good builder, but you could also be opening a can of worms in finding out you have received a booby prize of a builder.

So, really, you are **taking your pick**.

We are here to give you some keys to open the box and be able to give your money away when a good job has been done. There are loads of builders out there, as you know. We don't have all the answers. If anybody says they do have all the answers, me and Bruiser will go halves with them when they bottle it, because they will never have to work again when they start selling it.

Hey, me and Bruiser are qualified, experts, time-served old school builders, so coming to us would be a blessing sent from the main man above.

We are not the only good builders though. Trust me! Actually, we can find them and do the due diligence for you if you want; that will all depend on how successful this book is and what feedback we get from you. There are numerous ways we could help you, come to think about it. My mind is getting excited about how we could help you. Anyway, time will tell. You just have to be patient and help us to help you by giving us your feedback. Fair enough?

I digress again.

What do you mean; you don't know where to find good builders?

45

Now you have a starting point. Look, we shall give you our opinion. If we had the real 100% answer we'd bottle it too, and just keep counting the royalties coming in. The truth is nobody really knows, because they all have different opinions.

Hey, don't get fooled by the so-called experts. You know who they are. Go into any search engine on the internet, newspaper, etc. and they will appear, giving you their **expert** opinion. Type in 'builders' and words relating to it and see what comes up on the internet. Who are these people anyway? They have a website, give their titles or qualifications, and we **assume** they know what they are talking about.

Definition of an **Expert** from the *Oxford Reference Dictionary*:

Highly practised and skilful, or well informed in a subject (Page 286).

By the way, do you know what can happen when you assume? It makes an Ass out of You or Me (an <u>Ass</u> out of yo<u>u</u> or <u>me</u>.)

Don't be fooled by titles and qualifications; make sense? No! Yes? OK, look!

I don't know what your definition of an expert is, but as time has passed by in me and Bruiser's game, we have found these definitions to be highly debatable.

In most cases, the word **rubbish** would be a better term.

46

Yes, perhaps as me and Bruiser are getting older we may be getting more cynical, but it gives us the hump when titles and qualifications are used at times. They are just words, on pieces of paper. **Fact!**

I'm an A1 NVQ Assessor. Basically, I get people qualified and I know that, if I wanted to, I could get someone officially qualified in about 40 minutes.

How?

By taking a few photos, asking a few questions on an audio recorder, and building the portfolio in this way. And they would not need to have worked in that profession for me to do that. (It's not honest practice though).

What? You may be asking?

Look, I know organisations that can go to an employer and are able to get their employees qualified with an NVQ qualification to say they are competent, when they haven't even lifted a trowel, if it's in relation to bricklaying, for example.

So **prove it if you are qualified**, I say.

Again, don't get me wrong. I do believe there are real experts in their own fields and well-qualified people, like me and Bruiser, but we know the words **real experts** are used far too lightly at times.

Words such as time, pain, hard work, and age should

47

be used more to give credibility to the word expert.

Make sense?

Look, all I'm saying is, someone may be qualified, time-served or have passed an exam, but it doesn't necessarily make them any good at what they do!

I've had a poor doctor, dentist, teacher, and politician but I got rid of them.

Why? Because, in my opinion, they were not very good at what they did. So off they went!

Have you heard this quote before?

I told my doctor I broke my leg in two places. He told me to quit going to those places. Henry Youngman

Summary
- **Become Dick Tracy**
- **'Take your pick' with Michael Miles**
- **Go to your local pub**
- **Do your due diligence**
- **Never assume experts are experts**
- **Get them to prove their expertise**

SECTION 5:
The Six Ps

You may ask the question, what are you to do? Well, believe it or not, all is well.

"Hey Bruiser, I just had a vision of you coming to the rescue on your horse!"

Guess what Bruiser's reply was? Dick? You were correct!

Now, what I'm about to tell you may surprise, bewilder, or even frighten you. In fact, I may even go as far as to say that you may be thinking to yourself, you are having a laugh! Well, here goes.

It's you who has the answer to finding the ideal builder by following the six Ps:

Proper Prior Preparedness Prevents Poor Performance.

But don't panic, we are going to keep giving you guidance throughout this book. By the end of it, you will definitely be able to find a good builder on your own. Trust me!

We're not going to leave you on your own even when we get to the end of this book with you. As long as you want us to help, we shall give you our contact details.

What really annoys me and Bruiser is the fact that no matter how many times people watch programmes like *Cowboy Builders* on the TV, there are lots of you who continue to get ripped off. Hopefully, you will not be another one of those people because you are being educated now.

Here is a list of suggestions that we feel will definitely protect you.

- **Start with referrals when looking for a builder**
Friends and family are a good source, especially when they have already had work done by someone. Check the work out for yourself though, because people have different expectations as to what is good quality work.

- **Ask for references**
Ask whoever you contact for two or three references in relation to what previous work has been completed by them. Once you have the references, **make sure you definitely go and check them out.**

It amazes me and Bruiser how people don't bother to follow up on references; it seems people find reasons why they shouldn't do it. For example, people say to themselves, they must be OK because they wouldn't give references if they had something to hide.

Wrong!

Don't you think that shady builders would know that

51

the majority of people think this way? Think about it!

- **Find out if the builder belongs to a respected trade body**
  Me and Bruiser are suspicious of trade bodies and organisations that set themselves up to recommend tradespeople. Just make sure they are respected trade bodies. Make sure the builder's membership is up to date by giving the trade body a call. Again, some shady builders will get registered and then not maintain their membership. People sometimes fall for the membership sign they carry on their vehicles without checking to see if the builder is a member or not. The good thing about being a member of a respected body is that they will have required standards in place for the members to follow. If you are not happy with the standard of work you have had completed by the builder, you can go to the body and complain. Reputable builders don't want grief, so they make sure their work is of a good standard.

- A good website is http://www.direct.gov.uk. If you do have a problem from the Government recommend, you can at least go and give them some grief.

- **Agree the work and put pen to paper. Again, it's called a contract.**
  Make sure it outlines the work to be done, date of completion, security and safety arrangements, toilet facilities, where they are going to eat (if re-

52

quired), and hours of work, etc.

- **Deposits and payment**
Watch out when paying deposits. Deposits are only normally paid when specific materials are required for the job or when the job is going to take a long time to complete.
Otherwise, me and Bruiser would recommend that you avoid paying a deposit and agree any payments in writing.

- **Beware of the VAT scam**
VAT-free deals mean a couple of things. The builder doesn't earn enough earnings each year to be VAT registered. Or he's avoiding paying tax, in our opinion. Ask yourself questions such as will the builder be around long enough if there is need for any repairs to be done? Does the builder have a big enough firm to complete the job required? Can you have a valid contract if there is no proof of payment?

Just think about those questions before you go ahead and have someone take on a job for you. If these questions can be answered positively, you can make a decision from there.

Again, don't expect to find what you are looking for by what people have told you or by what me and Bruiser tell you. That way you won't be disappointed if it wasn't what you got or expected. **Make up your own mind!**

(Worth another read that).

If we were able to tell you

- What to do
- Where to go
- And how to do something

and you actually did that for the rest of your life with no problems; we would bottle it and sell it to every person in the world. (I like the term 'bottle it', as you've probably noticed by now).

As a parent, I would love to have developed a magic pill to give my children, and to have been able to protect and solve all of their problems. (Bear with me, I'm getting there). I know you are not looking for me and Bruiser to give you your life answers (again that's for another book), but the principles will be the same in finding your ideal builder.

What are they, you may be thinking. Well, here we go.

"Go over all that we have advised in this book and implement it, and you will find your ideal builder!"

Become an **expert.** (No, I'm not contradicting myself). This is an area you can strive to become an expert in.

Do what we have gone over, through

- Repetition
- Time
- Trial and error

and you will get there!

54

Did I hear you throwing the book across the other side of the room, or throw your toys out of the pram?

Please go and pick it up. (Again, bear with me!)

If you
- Go on the internet
- Look in the newspapers
- Go to organisations who have recommended tradesmen on their books
- Have recommends from friends, etc.

ultimately, the **choice will be yours**!

Have you ever had a recommendation from someone in relation to something that was important to you, only to find out you weren't happy or impressed with what you landed up with? Or you have decided to do something or go somewhere based on what you have read or heard, again to find out it wasn't all that it was cracked up to be? I know me and Bruiser have.

If you haven't experienced any of the above, you will at some time in life. **Inevitable!**

If you believe the doctors, nothing is wholesome; if you believe the theologians, nothing is innocent; if you believe the military, nothing is safe. **Lord Salisbury**

Guess what? That's the way it is. Some you win, some you lose. That's life!

The best advice we could give is try the way you feel comfortable with when looking for a good tradesman. We have discussed some places to look, but just keep your mind open to finding someone. Go with your feelings. You only have yourself to blame then. It's called taking responsibility!

Remember, when you find someone, go by your gut feelings and listen for the alarm bells to ring if you find the wrong one.

Ladies! I was asked by a woman some time ago what questions to ask when you are dealing with builders. Do you know what I said to her?

Go with your female intuition! That's your gift from God!

Let me explain. We blokes basically don't trust any bloke anyway; let's just say it's a man thing. I guess it's a base instinct we have in thinking whether he's a **friend or foe**. All I know is, when we come across one of our own species there is usually something we don't like about him. First instinct, you might say. Don't get me wrong, that can change when we get to know someone, but first impressions are what we go by. (By the way, this is just my opinion, not the rest of the male population's necessarily. I bet I'm not far wrong where most blokes are concerned though. Bruiser also agrees with me by the way).

Ladies, let me repeat what I said earlier. Go by your **female intuition**!

56

Look, I know that when you ladies have had contact with a bloke you have said, "I don't know what it is, but I wouldn't want to be left in the same room as him on my own." Am I right or wrong? There you go, I knew I was right! It's called female or women's intuition.

Whatever work you want doing, please do some research. There are plenty of DIY books that give you the basics on any of the building tasks you are likely to have done. Now you have the ultimate research book right here in your hands.

The same applies, for instance, in that you could ask what the builder would be doing and how he would be doing the work, and go and read up a little about it before the builder comes to do the job. Get a minimum of three opinions from different builders and see what they say. We are actually thinking about putting a provision on our website so that we can provide some advice and guidance in relation to problems arising, or better still preventing them, so you can go and receive some help from us. This is just a thought at the moment. We are thinking about providing a complete service to help you, the people. Again, we will need some feedback from you if this would be something you are interested in.

Ask direct questions and **look them in the eyes**.

You may be saying, "But I'll go bright red, I don't like looking strange men or women in their eyes and asking them questions, especially big buff builders and lovely lady builders".

57

Well our advice would be, just **do it**! It will save you a lot of money. Builders can be shy and go red as well. We all feel embarrassed at times. Don't forget when someone lies to you, their eyes always give them away.

Try this exercise with a friend. Ask them some questions and ask them to lie about some of the answers they give. See if you can guess the ones they are lying about and keep trying until you can tell by their eyes when they are telling the truth or lying. And KISS.

"What?!"

OK, please calm down. Stop screaming. Get some fresh air and have a sip of water before you faint. Take some deep breaths before I carry on. Are you OK?

Good. Then I shall carry on. I should have told you what KISS stands for, shouldn't I, before you began hyperventilating and nearing a heart attack. Forgive me, but if you could only have seen your face! **KISS stands for, Keep It Simple Stupid**. That's not intended to be rude, by the way; using the word 'stupid' just makes a point.

Look, if you have to do all of the above before you calm down and do what we've suggested it will save you a lot of money. Trust me, it's all a game. So, you need to learn to play the game. Remember, we builders call it the **building game**. That should give you a clue as to how you need to play it.

I know there are some of you saying, "Uh, if you think

it's funny when I lost all of my money, because you class it all as a game, I don't, I'm not amused, so there." Calm down. We're not classing it as a joke, but there are those out there who will take the mickey out of you where your pockets are concerned, if you aren't careful. That won't be funny, as some of you have already learnt. So give what me and Bruiser are suggesting a try and see if it works.

I remember a time when we were looking for some work and we were given the telephone number of a contractor to call. Now me and Bruiser didn't like driving around looking for work; we preferred to give contractors our interview techniques over the phone to know whether we were going to get ripped off or not. Now if we were able to speak to them personally it was even better. One look at Bruiser and there was no way we were ever going to get ripped off.

Guess what? We never did. Surprise, surprise! No, it wasn't a surprise really, bless old Bruiser.

I used my telephone technique when we were unable or too lazy to go travelling around. Would you like to hear what I said? This never failed for us either. I would be asking questions about the job, such as

- What was the contractor paying?
- How long was the job going to last?
- Who was the main contractor?

Then, as we were talking, I'd just ask the question out of the blue: **"Are you going to rip us off?"**

"What? Are you crazy? You can't say that! After all, it's not cricket, old boy!"

Let me tell you something. If I'm concerned that I'm going to get ripped off, I'm not going to wait to get ripped off before I find out if I am going to get ripped off. (Have another read of that statement).

Does that make sense?

Again, the way I saw it was, when you were on the phone their guard was down when talking to me. They were more open, I found, when you got into a conversation in most cases. Nobody expects to be asked a direct question in that way. Some would say that it would feel rude for them to ask that question, because the builder might feel offended. Well, would you feel offended and feel that it was rude if you got ripped off? Just a thought.

When I'd asked that question, I just listened for their response. If it went quiet and they had to think about the reply they were going to give before answering, sometimes with a little cough or something like that in between, then I heard the old **alarm bells** ringing in my head and the old **gut feeling** started churning over.

When they responded straight away with something like, "I tell you what, mate, you can come and speak to… or call… if you want to know how straight I am, etc." I was able to make a good judgement.

Again, does this make sense?

60

I didn't ask if you would feel comfortable if you had to ask what I've just suggested. Ask yourself, "What have you got to lose?" In our opinion, you have a lot to gain. It's your choice, that's all I'm saying. When me and Bruiser were working on the tools, we were able to notice the builders who were **chancers**, and the ones who weren't. How? By the way they

- Walked
- Carried their tools
- How they were dressed
- How they looked around the job

These were just a few of the ways we knew. I know you may be saying, "Well how could I tell? I'm not an experienced builder!" You may not be, but you have had life experiences when dealing and observing people. In fact, I would go as far as to say some of you are experts in that field, even though you may not be aware of it. It's a gift you may have. It's all the same really.

If you think you are useless at observing people or making decisions, then you still have choices. You can bury your head in the sand and get someone to do it for you, but be aware; you may have to blame someone for not getting it right for you. Or get a little uncomfortable and prove to yourself you can **feel the fear and do it anyway**! (Don't forget FEAR can mean False Evidence Appearing Real).

One of the effects of fear is to disturb the senses and cause things to appear other than what they are. **Miguel de Cervantes.**

61

Get **uncomfortable** and then it becomes comfortable. Act in spite of **fear, inconvenience, discomfort, uncertainty, anything**. Me and Bruiser believe in you! You've bought our book so you are a doer, in our opinion. Keep on reading and you will definitely become more confident in knowing **How to win when dealing with builders**.

Summary

- **Six Ps**
- **Start with referrals**
- **Ask for references**
- **Do they belong to a trade body?**
- **Government websites**
- **Have a contract**
- **Deposits and payments**
- **Beware of VAT scams**
- **Ask the questions**
- **The choice is yours**
- **Try the way you feel comfortable**
- **Go with your feelings**
- **Female intuition**
- **Look them in the eyes**
- **Ask direct questions**
- **Kiss (Keep It Simple Stupid)**
- **Telephone conversations**
- **Are you going to rip us off?**

SECTION 6:
Golden nuggets of information

The reason for getting you to think about what you should do to find a builder was for you to be able to think for yourself. We hope you found this useful.

Now we are about to give you a gift, and not just any gift. If you apply these principles in other areas of your life, you will become a lot happier than you are now.

Me and Bruiser know you are happy now because you are reading our book. (Come on, you must admit you have laughed at times).

We are going to offer you some **Golden nuggets** of information, on your quest of learning **How to win when dealing with builders**. Like any gift though, the only way you are going to benefit from it is by you receiving it. If you personally don't receive the gift and open it to see what's inside, how will you know what it is? Me and Bruiser have learnt that if we are given something valuable and haven't earnt it, it's more likely that we are not going to appreciate it.

Give a man a fish and you feed him for a day; teach a man to fish and you feed him for a life time. **Lao Tzu**

Me and Bruiser are becoming life builders now, I guess. We are in a position to share our knowledge with you. Just some people asking our opinion in relation to

64

building work was the reason for writing this book. I hope you notice we use the word 'book' a lot; we hope that you will read our information as a book and use it as **a guide** for yourself. We say guide because we want to help you, show you, to lead you. We've had to learn the hard way, just like a guide dog helps a blind person; we too want to help you.

By the way, do you know what another definition of the word luck is? Labouring Under Correct Knowledge. (Do you see it?) In our opinion, it's no coincidence that you have been directed to this book, you have been using correct knowledge principles to be guided to where you are now. It's no coincidence; it didn't just happen. You are the one who needs a pat on the back. Well done! (That's a pat on the back from me and Bruiser).

"Right, Bruiser, what is the first Golden nugget we're going to offer them?"

Gold!
Always believe in your soul
you've got the power to know
you're indestructible
always believe in, because you are
Gold
glad that you're bound to return
there's something I could have learned
you're indestructible, always believe in...[2]

---

2 The lyrics are from Spandau Ballet, a pop group of the 80s.

"Wow, steady Bruiser. Where did that come from? I'm impressed! Not with the singing, mind; talk about being tone-deaf."

Those lyrics from the song *Gold* are what we've been talking about really, aren't they? It's all about **you**. All you have to do now is believe it!

Oh, by the way, when it says in the lyrics "Glad that you're bound to return..." don't forget we need feedback from you. We want this book to be a big success. Hey, what about a bestseller? That would give us builders some cred in the book world, wouldn't it?

Bruiser's right, you know: you are **gold**. You're worth your weight in it, especially if you get it right. (Another book in the making...)

I know what Bruiser is referring to; you need to **think outside the box** when dealing with builders at times. You try pinning a plumber down: they can be your worst nightmare to get hold of or keep on a job. We say think outside the box, because that's what we're all living in.

No? Well, we shall see. Bear with me.

"What? How dare you!" I hear some of you saying. "I'm not a down and out; I don't live in a box!"

Again, bear with me. I always get there in the end, with the words of wisdom according to me and Bruiser.

Me and Bruiser have felt like **down and outs** at times,

66

when trying to keep the money coming in, when times have been hard. When dealing with builders, people will let you down at the last minute after promising you the earth. This can be very costly, if you're not careful.

Right, so are we living in boxes? We shall see.

What do you live in? Most people live in a house. Some people may live in a pigsty of a house, but that's their choice. Correct? So, what shape is the house? Let's say square or rectangular for the sake of argument. There you go, just like a **box!** I rest my case, your honour.

OK, perhaps not literally in a box, but can you see how we check this in the way we think? (Got you thinking though, didn't it?)

When we've watched TV, what do we say to each other when we talk about what we've been watching? How about, "Did you see what was on the box last night?" This is just an example.

"Well, I don't!" I hear some of you say. "We say television!"

There you go, it's called **thinking in boxes** again. When we go to the shops or supermarket, what do we see food packed in mostly? In **boxes!**

Everywhere we go we see them, so no wonder we think inside the box. There's big money in thinking about the TV box and watching it; advertisers love it. Most of the

67

population spend most of their time watching it. Come on, be honest, true or false? Hey, my case is getting stronger, your honour.

So, when considering **How to win when dealing with builders**, when thinking outside the box, here is what me and Bruiser would suggest you think about.

What about a **goldmine ad**?

"What's that?" I hear some of you say. Give me a chance; I'm just about to tell you.

I'm talking about putting your own ad in the newspaper, shop window, or on leaflets, for example, to advertise for your ideal builder for the job you want doing. **It's as simple as that!** Start thinking outside the box.

What do most people do when they want something? They look where the rest of the population looks, because they are all thinking inside the box.

It's called being programmed!

Me and Bruiser want you to get out of your comfortable chair watching the television box and start saving yourselves some time and money. Do the opposite to what everyone else is doing and you are thinking like the rich.

I'm sitting at my computer every day, writing this book now. Bruiser is having a nap most of the time; he says it's where most of his inspiration comes from, in his dreams, so he can then give me his pearls of wisdom when I ask him questions. I'm beginning to wonder, who has been the brain behind our partnership over the years? Bruiser may look dopey at times but, like I said, he's as sharp as a two edged sword. He doesn't lose much sleep; I'm the one doing that.

I've actually been writing this book from 5am each day and finishing at around 12 midnight, getting up again around 5am the following morning, to start over again. I'm trying to start at around 9am to be honest now, so I can get a balance. I often wake at 3am because thoughts for this book come to mind.

When I get up, I then go out for my one to two hour walk each day, which gives me time to have some exercise and think about what I want to say in this book. To get some inspiration, I guess. I get back home, have some breakfast, and back onto the computer again. I'm not telling you this to impress you, because I love doing what I'm doing, to be honest. I've found my **passion** in writing my thoughts and experiences down on paper, to try to help people like you. It takes effort and dedication.

How many of you are going to receive the gifts we are offering you? How many of you are going to do it? You will not have to put in the effort and dedication into writing this book; that has already been done for you. All you need to do is to put some effort into reading and applying the principles taught, and you've received the gift. Hopefully, we shall receive some of your success stories on how this book has helped you. Unfor-

69

tunately, not all of you will do it in relation to reading and applying the principles you are reading. That is one of those facts.

Oh well, I guess that gives more work and cash to me and Bruiser. We can do the things people don't want to do for themselves and be paid a fortune. Hey, I'm not having a go at you for not wanting to do it yourself, that's your choice. Remember though, I did say at the beginning of this book that it's mine and Bruiser's passion to try to help you. We are writing this book so that we can help you save a lot of money.

Fair enough?

Don't forget what I said at the beginning, this is a **gift** for you; it's up to you if you want to **open the box (book)** and take the gift out. Again, what do we receive gifts in? You've got it; it's called a **box**. (Or book).

Just think about the benefits in advertising for your ideal builder yourself: you can be in control of the work from day one. Actually, you are becoming the contractor; you say what your terms and conditions are. You can say what you are willing to pay and how much. That's down to the market conditions and how badly you want the work doing, or how much the builder wants the work.

Would you like to have another Golden Nugget?

If I were to tell you a way of getting work done by a professional person for nothing, you paying no money for

70

the work, would this be worth knowing?

Would you like to know?

How much would you be prepared to give me and Bruiser for that Golden Nugget of information? I bet you are not able to put a figure on it, are you? If you gave the figure that we have in mind you would probably say, "You're having a laugh, mate!" You snobs would probably say, "My dear boy, do you think I am a fool? I'm an educated person. Come on now, be more realistic!"

You know what Bruiser would say?

You've guessed it; I don't have to tell you, do I?

Actually, I was called an inverted snob once by an ex-girlfriend. I didn't know what it meant, to be honest. She was clever; she had a law degree and all that. She described an inverted snob as someone (me) having a thing against posh people. Well, that wasn't true if posh means that they speak nice; I haven't got a problem with that. I do have a problem if someone thinks they're better than someone else is, for whatever reason that may be. That gives me and Bruiser the hump, to be honest. In our opinion, we haven't walked in someone else's shoes, so who are we to look down on anyone? We all come into this world the same way and we shall all go out the same way. That's better, had my say, set the world to rights and got it off my chest. Besides, I take being called an inverted snob as a compliment, compared to what I have been called in my time.

71

Where was I? Oh, yes!

So, back to getting work done for nothing. The answer is "Wouldn't we all like to know? We would have cracked it!"

Hang on, hang on! We are going to give you the answer, because me and Bruiser want you to have the same goldmine of information that we have.

So, this is it!

I bet when I tell you the answer, you will say or think "Is that it?"

All the great ideas or inventions are obvious when we have been shown or told how to do something. Interesting that. They're always right under our noses.

OK, be patient!

I know you are waiting to go and bottle this information, and try to sell it to the highest bidder. And there's me and Bruiser just giving it away, for the price of this book. Bargain!

Well, here it is.

Find someone who is just starting out in the building game, is desperate to gain customers and trying to build a good reputation. They are looking to build a business. Now if you can offer that person some incentive, like recommendations to x amount of people and praising their work to those people, as an example, do you think they would be too concerned about doing something for you for nothing? How about if they were able to get referrals in return? What about if they thought they were going to receive much more back in return, are they likely to do something for free?

Don't try to rip people off with promises; promising to do something in return for them, if they are doing work for nothing for you. If you do try to rip people off, you are asking to receive some pain in one form or another. You don't want to put this option to the test. Again, **I guarantee** some form of pain would be coming your way if you did.

Look, there are people who are out there now, desperate to make an impression. They want to succeed. They want to make a name for themselves. If you have something they want, they will pay you for it, or give their time for **free**!

I remember when **Mike Tyson** was being interviewed and they asked him something to do with how much money he has available to spend when he goes out. Do you know what he said? He said,

> *When I was classed as a nobody, and living in the ghetto, there would be no chance for me to go into a shop or restaurant, and expect to get a free meal or any product for free. They wouldn't even let me into certain places. Now when I go to those places, they won't let me pay for anything, I can't give my money away to them, they won't take it!*

73

Why is that? Well, we believe it's because if people can see by not taking any money, under certain circumstances, and over the long term they are going to receive more money, they will not take any money. Fact! I told you it is too easy for you to get your head around. Well, maybe not for everyone: I can see the penny has dropped with some of you. Good for you! That's called **thinking outside of the box**.

Some of you are probably saying "What? Is that it?"

Yes, that's it. Another Golden Nugget for you!

So simple, really. But how many of you will actually go out and find someone to do the work you require for nothing? The rich and famous get these deals all the time. Trust me! They get people to pay for their business opportunities all of the time, without using their own money.

Again, that's a fact.

We understand how daunting it can be to change your way of thinking, and become the contractor instead of employing someone to do the work for you. It's all about thinking outside the box and doing it. Me and Bruiser have had to do things that have been uncomfortable many times, but once you do it once you've overcome an **imaginary fear** that doesn't really exist. You never look back. I hope this has given you something to think about.

What you focus on expands!

74

Many years ago, I was in a meeting and someone was using a metaphor of rowing a boat, in terms of becoming successful. He said, "The problem is, we are not all rowing in the same direction!" I replied, "Well if we are all heading towards a waterfall, we need to start rowing in a different direction!"

My point is, in most of our lives we all follow the rest of the population in whatever direction they are going, because we have been programmed to do so. What me and Bruiser have learnt is that when we have started to think outside of the box we have received more of the rewards.

Don't get me wrong, I'm not saying go and do something that will cause you financial pain or physical pain. What I'm trying to say is, just start to do something different each day that is a little **uncomfortable**. Once you do that, it becomes **comfortable**.

There is that old question: "Where do you find the best fruit?" Answer: "Out on a limb!"

My understanding of this is if you went out on the limb of a tree (branch) to the very end, you would find the best fruit. Why? Because that is where the best fruit will be found, due to it being more exposed to the sun light.

There are not many people who will go out on a limb, to get the best fruit, to where there is plenty of fruit available. In my opinion, that's the same with life opportunities; there are not too many people who will receive those gifts and go out on a limb and do something with them, unfortunately.

Give what you have been taught some thought, because it will help you with your quest in learning **How to win when dealing with builders**.

Summary
- **Receive the gift**
- **Labouring Under Correct Knowledge**
- **Think outside of the box**
- **Goldmine ads**
- **Work done for free**
- **What you focus on expands**
- **Out on a limb**

SECTION 7:
Working with The Terminator

"Bruiser, do you remember your mate Pillhead Phil from Rhyl, and his mate The Terminator?"

"Yes, it couldn't have happened to a nicer couple of dickheads, if you ask me!"

Now, here is a lesson on getting yourself protected, as I've mentioned earlier in the book. The Terminator was a contractor we came across many years ago, who was a real lowlife, to say the least. In fact, you've probably scraped better things off the bottom of your shoe.

Well, we were working on a job and came across some subcontractors who The Terminator tried to stitch up. He would get them to do work and then promise them more work if they did the work cheaper than someone else did. When the work was completed, he would just sack them. Hence his nickname The Terminator.

In those days, some shady contractors used to have their minders with them, just in case there was any trouble. The Terminator had his mate Pillhead Phil from Rhyl working for him as his hod carrier. Now Pillhead Phil was a body builder, on steroids. The problem with steroids is they help build muscle faster, but there are side effects. Pillhead Phil would suddenly go a little loopy. He would start throwing things about and shouting. This was the effects of the steroids.

Me and Bruiser have had contractors say they weren't going to pay, but after Bruiser had a word in their ear they always paid without fail. That's the way it was in those days; you had a word in their ear or hoped for the best in being paid for work you had done. Now The Terminator wasn't silly enough to upset Bruiser. Neither was Pillhead Phil.

Bruiser gets on with most people, but these two were not on his Christmas card list. Anyway, The Terminator thought he'd be especially kind to these subcontractors, due to it being almost Christmas.

So, he waited until the Monday, for them to come back to the job, before he gave his famous words, "You're fired!"

He lived up to his title of The Terminator. He just loved to be able to upset someone. He had Pillhead Phil with him, so there was little point in most blokes looking for a **Rumble in the Jungle**[3]. Pillhead Phil was a big bloke, but once he started lifting weights his muscles would start pumping up and he'd be as stiff as a board. Anyway, on this occasion The Terminator had a shock. All that the sub- contractors said was "You can't do that, we do have rights!"

Now this wasn't heard of before by most builders. We always had the impression that if you were a subcontractor, you were classed as self-employed and had no rights. If we were given the sack, we might go and plot

---

3 The Rumble in the Jungle was the name of a famous boxing fight between Muhammad Ali and George Foreman in 1974.

our revenge or just take losing our job as part of working in the building game.

The next time we saw the sub- contractors was some weeks later on another site. I asked them what happened in relation to being paid by The Terminator. "We got paid. Our union was going to take him to a tribunal if he didn't pay up, and once The Terminator knew this, he paid up."

I know the law is changing all the time, but this was the first me and Bruiser had heard about unions for the self-employed. Those days are gone, when you had to put up with not being paid for work that had been done or getting help and support with legal work if you needed it. So, you punters, and builders for that matter, reading this book, go and **do your due diligence**: get yourselves protected from being **terminated** in one form or another. You don't have to go through solicitors paying extortionate fees to get yourselves protected.

Have a look at your house insurance policy, for instance. There will be sections in there where you can have legal protection, in the form of advice and support. Take a look. I'm not saying what you should or shouldn't do: that is up to you, but that is an option.

Was that useful? I hope so. Again, I want you to get the picture: as I've stated before, we remember things better by stories and pictures. **Protection is so important!** Protection gives you peace of mind, which will lead to happiness.

80

Summary

- **Get yourself protected**

SECTION 8:
How to prevent painful things happening

Someone asked me once, "If you have a pain, what do you want it to do?" "I want it to go away!" He then said, "Well, become a good pain!"

I mentioned, near the beginning of the book, about pain and what we basically want as human beings. That is to be happy. Well, sometimes we don't learn, do we? We keep on doing the same old things, and the same old problems rear their ugly heads.

What we mean by becoming a good pain is to be **consistent** and **persistent** until you get what you want. Let me share with you another story; this took place when Bruiser had the Gypsy Jim problem. (Now that Bruiser isn't around at the moment, I can carry on without bringing back eye-watering memories for him).

Well, it was that time in Bruiser's life when bad pain seemed to follow him around. He seemed to have a couple of months where grief was his constant companion. Now if grief was Bruiser's best friend, then the people who were causing it also now know what **Bruiser grief** was all about. You see, we were still on the same job at Crick, just after Gypsy Jim had been rushed to hospital for causing poor old Bruiser grief.

Now Giuseppe came from Italy. He wasn't a very tall man; in fact, he would be deemed small, just over five feet small, to be precise. Now it has been mine and Bruiser's experience that once you give some men a little authority it can, unfortunately, go straight to their head. From the time Giuseppe had been promoted to a charge hand, his character seemed to quickly change. Now, bearing in mind he was a very small man, he probably always dreamt of being a big man: besides, they couldn't get anyone else to take the job.

Now, after probably being picked on at school, or being called names most of his life, Giuseppe's dream had come true: it's called having **power**! You see, Giuseppe was becoming a bit of a dictator. That is where Giuseppe's new name, Mussolini, evolved from.

Mussolini very quickly upset a lot of people, due to his little man syndrome, which caused this abnormal condition to take control of him. Well, Mussolini upset Bruiser on a Friday, as I recall, and this would be a day Mussolini would probably never forget. Poor old Bruiser had been struggling all week with his prized assets giving him grief, in the form of painful throbbing. Bruiser was taking some medication for the problem, in the form of paracetamol, but, unfortunately for Mussolini, it wasn't working. Also, please bear in mind that poor old Bruiser had been driven to drink the night before, due to his prized asset problem. Again, I warned Mussolini that if he had a problem with any of our work just to inform me and not bother Bruiser. But my advice wasn't heeded.

Mussolini decided to take on Bruiser, in the form of giving him verbal grief. I believe that Mussolini viewed

84

Bruiser as a modern day Goliath, knowing that David, the smaller man, wins the contest. Unfortunately, Bruiser was not only suffering from throbbing prized assets, but also had a throbbing headache due to a severe hangover. Bearing in mind, we were 30 feet above the ground working on scaffold at the time Bruiser's head went. He picked Mussolini up by the scruff of his neck, lifted him over the scaffold at arm's length and said, "If you come near me again, I'll drop ya!"

Now, have you heard the term that a person is **full of hot air**? Well, this was the time I finally witnessed what that meant. There seemed to be prolonged sounds of hot air coming from the posterior of Mussolini, as he was dangling at the end of Bruiser's arms. Let me say with my hand on heart, I am not a gambling man, but I swear that if Bruiser had let go of Mussolini, I bet he would have taken off! Bruiser then put Mussolini back onto the scaffold and carried on working as if nothing had happened.

It brought tears to my eyes, to think how Bruiser had progressed over the years. I was so proud of him; he hadn't dropped Mussolini. Other than Mussolini having to make a swift exit to the gents' toilet, it seemed to have had a positive effect on him. Surprisingly enough, he was a changed man after that experience. So, what have we learnt? **Respect** and **communication** are key ingredients to preventing pain. Remember that old saying "**Prevention is better than cure!**" I'm sure Mussolini would agree with me on that, as well as Gypsy.

You don't have to find yourself in Mussolini's situation

85

and be left to sort out a possible serious problem. If you have done your due diligence and communicated in the right way there shouldn't be a problem.

Look, we all have our bad days and problems; that's life. It's how we deal with them that are the key factors. Mussolini wasn't aware of Bruiser's problems. When he thought he would try to show a little bit of power, we know what the result was. Me and Bruiser have found that when you try to find a solution in solving a problem, without getting silly, you eventually get your rewards.

Never take life seriously; nobody gets out alive anyway. **Unknown**

If you have a problem arise with your builder, make sure you follow the grievance procedure. If you haven't agreed a grievance procedure with your builder, don't moan when you feel some painful exchanges coming your way. As I said earlier, write down what is expected in the agreement and don't forget it needs to be a win-win situation for both of you.

Man invented language to satisfy his deep needs to complain. **Lily Tomlin.**

Remember, it seems to be human nature to complain, for whatever reason.

There are three sides to an argument, your side, my side, and the right side. **Unknown**

86

Disputes are a massive money spinning business for lawyers; they're the only true winners. We've known people waste a lot of money, just so they can say they have won the battle. The sad thing is, they usually go on and lose the war. If things go wrong you can normally find that it was your own fault.

How?

Look, if you go down the blame road, you are not going to make anyone happy, including yourself. If you accept that whatever happens in life it is your choice on how you deal with it, you won't go far wrong. What I'm saying is, we all **choose** to be offended, nobody forces us to be.

Make sense?

I'm not saying it is easy to walk away from certain situations, but it is a choice we make. It will save you a lot of money. Trust me! By the way, I'm not trying to preach to you, I'm just telling you the way me and Bruiser have learnt to deal with things as time's gone by. If you don't agree, that's fine. It's called **free agency**. I believe in that. Just be mindful of the consequences though.

Victims:
- Blame
- Justify
- Complain

So, become the **victor**. Rich, successful people say, "I

create my life!" Other people believe that life happens to them. What you focus on expands.

Set some goals:
- No complaining for seven days
- Start taking full responsibility for what happens in life

Now these are a couple of goals me and Bruiser have found to be important, for us to become happier people. Hey, if this doesn't make sense to you, well don't do it! We are only going to tell you the things that will not ultimately hurt you, from our own life experiences. But the proof is in the pudding, as they say. I know I've spent a lot of time on pain vs. happy situations, but that is what it is all about, when you get down to it.

Summary
- **Be consistent and persistent**
- **Don't become power crazed**
- **Respect and communication are keys to happiness**
- **Prevention is better than cure**
- **Find a solution without getting silly**
- **Don't take life too seriously**
- **Choose not to be offended**
- **What you focus on expands**

SECTION 9:
Daktari Sue

We just want you to be happy and to avoid pain!

Here is a happy story; this is to do with Bruiser's second love (actually it was his third love). Her name is Daktari Sue. How did the name Daktari Sue come about? How come she was his third love, you may be asking? Well, I would have been his first love (again, not literally) and his second love would have been his pet canary.

Bruiser is an animal lover, you see, and he used to breed canaries. He had a favourite pet canary, and named her Dickie Bird. Why? Well, your guess is as good as mine. Yes, Bruiser named her Dickie Bird! Sweet, really.

But, back to Daktari Sue. Now me and Bruiser had just finished a shift on site and, it being Friday, we were making our way to town. We were just walking to the top of the stairway leading to the taxi rank near the bus station when we got this almighty smell of glue. As we walked around the corner, we came across a woman with a bag full of glue that she was sniffing.

Back in those days, there seemed to be a trend where glue sniffing became a social activity. Anyway, as we got closer to the woman, she obviously heard us coming and lowered the bag from her face. All I heard from Bruiser was Daktari. He was smitten. Yes, you could say it was love at first sight for Bruiser.

If Dickie Bird and her friends were there at the time, they would be flying around Bruiser's head; that was how bad it was. Daktari was a TV series in the 60s; it followed the work of Doctor Tracy, his daughter Paula, and his staff, who frequently protected animals from poachers and local officials.

When Bruiser saw the woman's eyes, she instantly reminded him of his favourite animal in the series. It never ceases to amaze me how Bruiser views things. Don't get me wrong, she wasn't ugly - after all, she is someone's daughter - but I couldn't see past the acne.

This woman obviously had an addiction and it was seemingly causing her to have severe acne on her face. What she was wearing didn't help either. It was a hot day and I could understand why she was wearing a t-shirt, but there are certain things that really annoy me; one of them is to do with combing your hair, especially when it comes to a woman.

I don't know about you, ladies, but your hair is one of your most beautiful features, in my opinion. I believe that for most of you it is something you take quite seriously. Well, on this day this woman had let the side down. Look, all I'm saying is when you have the mass of hair she had, wearing a T-shirt was not flattering her, in my opinion. She would have been better wearing a cardigan or some other form of clothing.

Ladies, I'm sure there are a number of you who would have at least tried to comb your hair, especially when it is under both of your armpits. Yes, the poor woman had

91

more hair underneath her armpits than she seemed to have on top of her head. It was a sad sight, really. As I stated previously, a short back and side's haircut would have made all the difference with all that hair, I feel. She certainly made up for what Kojak was missing at the time[4]. If she had shaved the facial hair she had, I feel it would have made all the difference. She did have a great handlebar moustache though; I must give credit where credit is due.

Anyway, getting back to why she reminded Bruiser of his favourite animal in the programme. You see with the hair on her face and her eyes being cross-eyed when she looked at us (it must have been the glue); she reminded Bruiser of Clarence the cross-eyed lion.

Again, I must reiterate that she wasn't an ugly person, even though you couldn't really tell. When she finally put her false teeth in, she did have a lovely smile. She obviously had a weight problem, which also didn't help. She was probably around 17 stone. The reason I could estimate her weight is because me and Bruiser, being the gentlemen we are, tried to help her to her feet, but, due to her profuse sweating, it was like trying to lift a large piece of lard off the ground, with her slipping through our fingers.

(Please be patient with me. I shall get to the point shortly, after finishing this happy story. There are morals to it.) At that moment, unexpectedly, came a woman who would later be known as Sticky Vicky, Daktari

---

4 Kojak was an American television series of the 70s. The main character was a bald New York police detective lieutenant played by the actor Telly Savalas.

Sue's best friend, we learnt. Why did we call her Sticky Vicky? Well, me and Bruiser had learnt that the woman and her best friend worked together as night workers. Sticky Vicky proudly informed us of this; and these are her actual words.

"Hello, my name is Victoria, and Sue and I are best friends. We have worked together in our profession most of our working lives. We are well-known around here, as the ladies of the night shift!"

I tell you what, and I'm not joking, the smell Sticky Vicky was giving off was like rotten eggs. Sticky Vicky would have been given a wide berth by a skunk! It will become clearer as we continue why she had this smell. She then asked me and Bruiser if we'd give them a lift back to their place of work, because it's normally the time they should be starting.

I don't know about you, lads, I've been asked a number of things in my time but never to take a couple of ladies of the night back to their place of work during working hours. It made me feel a little uncomfortable, to say the least. To be honest, Bruiser was getting quite excited at this point, due to the thought of spending some of the night with his ideal girlfriend. I was talked into it by all three of them, so off we went. From that moment on, Daktari Sue was the name I attached to our glue-sniffing lady of the night shift.

We finally arrived at their place of work. A large Rastafarian man opened the car door and greeted us with a smile from a Colgate advert. He shook mine and Bruiser's hands and seemed very happy to see Daktari Sue and Sticky Vicky finally turn up for work. He greeted them as if they were his girls and we learnt that he had been employing them for a number of years. Sorry, I forgot to tell you his name: it was Snowy White. They had been working together for a number of years and they were like family, it seemed. To be honest, you wouldn't have wanted to get on the wrong side of Snowy White either, especially if he was expecting money from you.

Me and Bruiser learnt that evening that Pearly (we re-named him Pearly because of his sparkling white teeth) had formed his company just after he had left school and saw an opportunity in employing mostly ladies who were prepared to work nights for him. It was on a self-employed basis, where he took a cut of the earnings they made. I suspect you are putting two and two together by now and seeing what sort of business they were in.

So, what profession were they in? Go on then; I'll give you the clues again:

- Daktari Sue's addiction to glue
- Sticky Vicky
- Night workers
- Self-employed basis
- Employer who looks after them

Go on, three guesses. I bet you got it in one!

Answer: "They were glue factory workers; they worked with glue!"

94

Well done, I'm impressed. I told you that you would get the answer in one. It's so easy to put two and two together in relation to people, isn't it, especially when you have the clues in front of you. First impressions are always the most important, don't you think?

Just think about the statements I've given you for a moment, please. Did you guess first time what Daktari Sue and Sticky Vicky did for a living? Don't forget what you have been taught and what you will continue to be taught throughout this book.

- **Never judge a book by its cover**
- **Don't assume, don't pre-judge**
- **Find out the facts first**
- **Do your due diligence**

When you apply the statements above you will save yourself a lot of possible embarrassment, money, and unnecessary pain, to mention but a few.

Make sense? Great!

I bet you can see where Sticky Vicky came from now. Yes, it was due to me and Bruiser shaking her hand for the first time and literally feeling like our hands were stuck to hers. The smell she had was due to the strength of the glue, which left the smell as a perfume on her clothing. We learnt that Pearly was incorporating the correct extraction system and good health and safety practice in the factory in general, so it was a healthy and safe environment for his girls to work in. Poor old Daktari Sue had an allergic reaction to the

95

glue and it caused her to have a skin condition, which was being successfully treated.

The sad thing was that the treatment was causing her body to have a hormone imbalance, which caused her to have too much hair growth and contributed to her weight problem. How sad that for whatever reason she chose to get into glue sniffing. We have all made wrong choices in life and she has eventually been able to turn her life around, I'm very happy to say.

We also met Daktari Sue and Sticky Vicky's friend Marion 'Nelly' Nelson, a female wrestler. Me and Bruiser would love to tell you more about the time we all got together at Pearly's work's do, but again that's up to you with the feedback we receive. Time does not permit us to reminisce now, unfortunately.

Actually, me and Bruiser would love to keep in touch with you and share our life stories and experiences with you. Just think; you could become part of our own extended family. **We need your feedback though!**

What have we learnt? Two and two does make four when you put the correct numbers together. We do assume at times, don't we? I think it's one of the main problems we have to overcome when learning **How to win when dealing with builders**. All is not what we sometimes think we see or hear.

When me and Bruiser first saw Daktari Sue we could have classified her as another down and out. All I know is, no matter what someone has done or become, we

96

haven't walked in their shoes (as I've stated before). Who are we to judge? The sad thing is our own life situation could change overnight and we could find ourselves with similar or worse problems.

The one thing we must do when learning **How to win when dealing with builders** is to try to get as many facts as possible, so that we can make an educated guess in relation to what we do or don't do.

Summary
- **Don't pre-judge**
- **Get the full picture**
- **Find out the facts**

How to win when dealing with builders

SECTION 10:
Be careful where you put your finger

As I said at the beginning of this book, Bruiser was a hod carrier before he took up the noble art of bricklaying. Now when you are learning any profession or lesson, there is a process we all have to go through. That process is **paying your dues**.

We can't avoid it. I bet you have all had to go through it in the past. If you haven't yet you've got it to come. It's like walking; we can't remember how many times we had to fall down and get back up before we started to walk, can we? Oh OK, I knew there would be someone. There's always someone who thinks they can remember. Well done! I bet you still count each step you take even now. Oh well, whatever turns you on.

Seriously though, we can't remember the pain we went through before we could take our first steps and be able to walk, can we? Look at us now; we walk without even thinking about it. I guess it's the law of life. **Before there's a gain, there's some form of pain.**

There's an old saying, I'm sure a lot of you have heard: **"No pain, no gain!"**

Well, would you like to hear about Bruiser's pain to fame? It's one of those famous stories that follow us throughout life. "Bruiser, do you remember your run in with PC Nick Nick, as you called him? No, not the two

99

fingers you're putting up to me. It was just the middle one, wasn't it?"

We're going back to Daktari Sue days and when Bruiser was at his peak, to be honest. He is without doubt the best hod carrier I've ever worked with. In those days a good hod carrier would keep two house plots loaded out with bricks and blocks so that the bricklayers would not run out of something to do.

For those of you who don't have a clue what I'm talking about, just be patient; it will be worth the wait.

Now Bruiser was in a good mood because it was another Friday afternoon and he was looking forward to seeing his Tweety Pie, Daktari Sue. The name Tweety Pie is not a problem with me; I know Daktari Sue has been called worse in her time, no doubt. Besides, Bruiser was happy; that was the main thing.

Bruiser was in the final chorus of I *did it my way* by Frank Sinatra. Then, all of a sudden, a loud scream from Bruiser's mouth. "Geronimo!" could be heard reverberating back to where we were standing. This was due to the echoing having no route of escape once it had made its way around the site. In my opinion, it was Bruiser's way of releasing a bad memory that had caused another painfully deep and traumatic psychological problem for Bruiser's subconscious to have to deal with. Like I said, I must tell you about what happened to him another time; it is so funny.

100

At that moment in time, I had a flashback to when Bruiser had been kicked in his prized assets by Gypsy Jim. Please spare a thought for my dilemma. I had already let him down in not doing what most parents would do in painful circumstances (just to remind you, rub or kiss the pain away). "Oh no, was Gypsy on the scene once again?" I was thinking to myself. Well this time when I went and looked to see what had happened to Bruiser, my worst fears seemed to manifest themselves before my eyes, because Bruiser had his hands between his legs. This time he didn't look knock-kneed and bowlegged though. I looked around and couldn't see any other person with him.

Was this a good or bad sign? There was a hole next to Bruiser; I had a vision of someone laying prostrate in it. Oh no, I thought, he hasn't killed someone has he? The same look was on Bruiser's face: pain, disbelief, anguish, all rolled into one it seemed. I should have known it wasn't his prized assets this time, because he was dancing around in a circle as well. I couldn't quite work out what he had done to be honest, because he was holding underneath his armpit as well.

"Bruiser, what have you done?" I asked.

"What do you mean, what have I done? Can't you see what I've done?" It never ceases to amaze me what we all say under these circumstances.

Once I saw him putting his hand in a bucket of water, I knew what he had done. I've been there myself on several occasions. What I found out after the dancing had stopped was that he had dropped a dozen bricks on his middle finger. Now that hurts! Again, I could see tears in Bruiser's eyes and his bottom lip had turned red due to him biting on it so hard. This wasn't the time to say, "It could have been worse, it could have been me!" It had crossed my mind but I thought better of it.

Did you know that when we laugh due to someone hurting themself it's because psychologically we're thinking "glad it wasn't me"? It's the slapstick comedy situation that comes out, apparently. Makes sense to me. I've dropped bricks on my finger before and, let me tell you, I was definitely glad it wasn't my finger now.

This wasn't the time to inform Bruiser of what I've just told you, because he would not have been amused. All he kept saying to me was, "I don't know where to put it; I don't know where to put it!" Whilst jumping up and down. Now there was one place that flashed through my mind, where I bet Bruiser hadn't thought of putting his finger, but I decided not to suggest that to him. He may have decided to put his trowel, with regards to me, in the same place I was thinking of suggesting for him to put his finger. The thought makes my eyes water!

I want you to get these pictures and stories in your mind's eye, so that you will remember what there is to learn. To be honest, I enjoy telling the stories anyway. It brings back many funny memories to me. My sick sense of humour, I guess. Come on, you have to see the funny side to them as well.

102

Now, we had a nurse who was on site so we made our way to her office, since Bruiser's finger was swelling up. We named her Florence, because of Florence Nightingale[5]. We loved Florence; she was a brick! (A brick in this context means someone who is solid and reliable). The building site we were working on was like fighting in the Crimean war at times. I don't know if we could class our Florence an Anglican but she was a saint at times; she had to be, to put up with builders on site.

Bruiser had dropped the bricks on the end of his middle finger of his right hand, right on his nail. The reason he had done this was because when he had taken the hod full of bricks off his shoulder and was placing them on the ground, he didn't move his finger out of the way quickly enough. Unfortunately, poor old Bruiser had a dozen bricks crash down on his finger.

A **hod** is a tool we place 12 bricks in at a time, so that they can be put onto the hod carrier's shoulder and then carried. The hod has a long wooden handle attached to an open bucket-like container. The bricks could then be carried up and down ladders and wherever the hod carrier wants to take them. There was a skill in removing the hod full of bricks off the shoulder and placing them in stacks on the ground wherever the brickwork was being built.

Florence wasn't there when we went to see her. What a

5 Florence Nightingale (12 May 1820 – 13 August 1910) was a celebrated English nurse, writer, and statistician. An Anglican, Nightingale believed that God had called her to be a nurse. She came to prominence for her pioneering work in nursing during the Crimean war, where she tended to wounded soldiers. She was dubbed the lady with the lamp after her habit of making rounds at night).

103

nightmare! Bruiser had definitely lost it; he was throwing his toys out of the pram and acting like a big baby. Actually he was trying to suck his finger so that the pain would go away, which made him look even more of a baby. But the heat from his mouth only made it worse. The only thing that gave him comfort was putting his finger in the cold bucket of water and this was only temporary pain relief.

There were times when I could have hit Bruiser over the head with my lump hammer; due to the grief he was giving my eardrums. What a dilemma! All we could do was to make our way home.

It didn't help that we were a couple of hours away from home and it meant going on the M25. Now travelling on the M25 on a Friday afternoon is definitely something to be avoided. All Bruiser could say was that he wished his Tweety Pie was there to comfort him. Guess what? I wished his Tweety Pie was there as well, even though she brought her own special body odour with her. The body odour was a mixture of perspiration and glue.

So, off we went down the motorway. Actually, I was surprised to see that the traffic on the motorway was quite clear for a Friday. I like to think we were being watched over by someone from up above, who was taking pity on us. Bruiser found a comfortable way of holding his finger as we were travelling along, which was good; at least he wasn't moaning and groaning so much when it was in that position. He kept his finger pointed in the air and the end of his finger was being pointed up-

104

wards so that the blood wasn't flowing downwards towards his nail. Well, that was the theory. I don't know if this was actually happening, but it seemed to be working for Bruiser and that was all that mattered.

Back in those days, it was no different from today really; people take offence at the smallest thing. As I said, it all boils down to how we see things at a given time. The word **hindsight** seems to rear its head on these occasions. How many times have we heard it said, "If only we knew then what we know now?" We would still probably do the same things. Yes, we would! I bet you would.

Think about it. The reason I'm saying this is that PC Nick Nick was in the position to cause Bruiser some more grief due to being a police officer. Unfortunately, he was seeing one thing and one thing only: an arrest was due.

Now I can understand how PC Nick Nick could get some things wrong on the spur of the moment, but the incident he referred to in his report was a little dicky to say the least. Bruiser has got me at it now: where the word 'dicky' has suddenly come from, heaven knows. "What a muppet I am!" I think after all of this; I needed to have a lay down as well.

So what actually happened? Bruiser was not a happy bunny as you can imagine. Luckily, we had Bruiser's favourite CD with us so he decided to play this song to give him some comfort. What is Bruiser's favourite CD and song, you may ask? Well, it was from *The Jungle Book*

105

and I'll give you a clue; Bruiser has the characteristics of the character who is also singing the song. Remember who I said Bruiser looked like? Well here are some of the lyrics to the song:

The Bare Necessities
Look for the bare necessities
The simple bare necessities
Forget about your worries and your strife
I mean the bare necessities
Old Mother Nature's recipes
That brings the bare necessities of life...
Lyrics by Terry Gilkyson

Yes, Bruiser was trying to put things into perspective and see life differently at that moment in time. It was admirable of him, in my opinion, and he was even trying to sing along with his lookalike, old Baloo. (Go online, type the song into Google, and listen to it. Think of Bruiser: you will have a laugh).

I must admit that the music as we were travelling along was quite loud. Normally I wouldn't like it that loud, but I didn't mind because, rather than listen to Bruiser feeling sorry for himself, I was willing to make the sacrifice. Little did we know that for the last couple of miles, PC Nick Nick was in the fast lane trying to get our attention. He was unable to get out of that lane due to the build-up of traffic, which didn't help because he kept moving back and forth. As we moved forward, he moved back; we moved back and he came to the side of us. You get the picture.

106

The only way I knew something was happening was because I saw a flash out of the corner of my eye. As I looked over, I could see PC Nick Nick with his head out of his passenger's side window taking a photo of Bruiser, as we were at that moment stationary. I thought, "Why anyone would want to take a photo of Bruiser and risk breaking their camera is beyond me, Bruiser being so good looking?"

"What was going on?" I thought. At this moment, Bruiser was looking over at PC Nick Nick and wasn't giving off good vibes. Bruiser doesn't take kindly to someone giving him verbal, even if it is from the long arm of the law. PC Nick Nick was shouting something to Bruiser that we couldn't understand, but we were able to pull over as requested. As I stated previously, Bruiser is a man of few words at the best of times and when he's receiving pain he speaks even less. The officer made his way around to Bruiser's side and gestured for Bruiser to wind his window down. Bruiser was unable to do this because of the swelling and throbbing that was still going on within his finger.

For the life of me, I couldn't see how PC Nick Nick couldn't see Bruiser's finger raised in the air and the look of pain on his face; I was really surprised, to be honest. It seemed that because Bruiser couldn't wind his window down, PC Nick Nick got even more annoyed.

Me and Bruiser thought he was on a power trip. The next thing we knew, PC Nick Nick came around to my side of the car and, once I was able to wind down my window, he informed us that we were nicked. He read us our rights and informed us that if we said anything this may be used in a court of law against us. At this point Bruiser replied, "What's going on, you dickhead?" PC Nick Nick turned bright red in the face. What Bruiser had said seemed to have hit a nerve. Bruiser had finally managed to get out of the car and PC Nick Nick suddenly realised the size of the problem, of Bruiser that is. I could see the colour draining from PC Nick Nick's face.

Bruiser still had his finger in the air, which was a blessing, because if he hadn't I dread to think what he would have done. At this point, the cavalry had also arrived, in the form of PC Tweedle Dee and PC Tweedle Dumb in their Panda car. Their arrival was causing quite a stir; what with Bruiser standing there with his finger in the air and three PCs standing looking at him. I noticed none of them seemed to know what to say or do next. There were cars going by sounding their horns and cheering Bruiser, for some reason.

Within a short period, me and Bruiser were escorted by the Keystone Kops to the local police establishment. On entering, we were finally questioned by the desk sergeant who began asking me and Bruiser questions in relation to the allegation that Bruiser had been giving PC Nick Nick some abuse, in the form of his middle finger being pointed in the air at him.

We were informed that the gesticulation was being performed by Bruiser for the past couple of miles on the M25, prior to our arrest. The desk sergeant stated

108

that under the circumstances these were serious allegations and asked what we had to say about it. He informed us that they also had photographic evidence on the Kodak instamatic camera, which he was in the process of showing me and Bruiser, and that there was the likelihood of a prosecution taking place.

Now this wasn't making Bruiser's finger any better, as the excitement was increasing Bruiser's blood pressure and thus making his finger feel even more painful. If someone had asked me and Bruiser why he had his finger in the air in the first place, we could have avoided this unfortunate predicament. I believe the fact that Bruiser was unable to inflict possible grievous bodily harm to someone at that time was a blessing, to say the least. I could see that I needed to make things clear to them before it got really silly.

The fact that I was able to inform them of the error of their ways, and for them to see the publicity implications that could have a detrimental effect on Her Majesty's constabulary, seemed to do the trick. There seemed to be a change of tone from that moment on, which resulted in a logical outcome: **freedom** is the word I'm looking for. I also informed them that I would be requesting to speak to a superior officer to lodge a formal complaint, which seemed to seal the acquittal before the trial.

PC Nick Nick wasn't a popular person at that moment in time. As is always the case, someone has to take the fall to save face and he was to be it. He was informed by his superiors that an apology was in order to me

109

and Bruiser for the waste of time and emotional stress we had suffered, due to PC Nick Nick being far too hasty in his summation of the situation. This seemed to cheer Bruiser up, since he didn't like PC Nick Nick from the start. That's why we nicknamed him PC Nick Nick, because we could see that he was a copper who enjoyed power.

PC Nick Nick was also given the pleasure of our company in taking me and Bruiser to the A&E department at the local hospital, so that Bruiser's finger could be treated. A nurse at the hospital was able to release the pressure of blood that was under Bruiser's nail, by piercing the top of his nail with a needle. This brought immediate relief from the pain Bruiser was under. He wanted to kiss the nurse in question, before he came to his senses. The nurse was a male nurse, you see. To be honest, I don't think the nurse would have minded; he seemed to take a shine to our Bruiser.

This is Bruiser's famous story on how he got away with putting his middle finger in the air to Her Majesty's constabulary for a number of hours. He even received a copy of a photograph from a workmate, who had received it from one of the people who was passing by on the motorway at the time of the incident. The motorist had taken a photo of Bruiser standing there gesticulating with his finger in the air, it seemed, with the three police officers looking at him in dismay. Bruiser actually had photographic evidence, which gave him more credibility. He definitely made the most of his fame, trust me!

110

Me and Bruiser were soon on our way back down the motorway so that he could be reunited with his beloved Tweety Pie. (I can't believe I'm calling someone Tweety Pie). Bearing in mind I had to put up with Bruiser singing one of his favourite songs from The Jungle Book earlier in the day, I now had to put up with another song he found appropriate to kill as we were travelling. Guess what this song was called? You will never guess in a million years; a lot of you wouldn't have even been born when this song came out.

It was called *Happiness*, by Ken Dodd.

(By the way, all of the songs I've mentioned in this book can be listened to if you Google the song names. Definitely worth a listen, and when you do picture Bruiser).

Here is part of the lyrics to the song:

Happiness.
> *Happiness, happiness, the greatest gift that I possess*
> *I thank the Lord I've been blessed*
> *with more than my share of happiness*
>
> *To me this world is a wonderful place*
> *and I'm the luckiest human in the whole human race*
> *I've got no silver and I've got no gold*
> *but I've got happiness in my soul*
>
> *Happiness to me is an ocean tide*
> *or a sunset fading on a mountain side*
> *a big old heaven full of stars up above*
> *when I'm in the arms of the one I love…*

Lyrics by Bill Anderson

111

Guess who Bruiser's thinking about here? It starts with 'T'. You've got it, Tweety Pie. So what do we learn from all of this? Well, I guess, **be careful where you put your finger**, especially when placing a dozen bricks on the ground. Do you know what I've learnt in life? **Avoidance is better than cure!** Not in all cases, I might add, but definitely in most cases. Look, you can't avoid the inevitable, whatever the inevitable is. For instance, we are getting older each day (I don't look it though!); the sun is always shining behind the dark clouds; I could go on and on. (Actually, I might at some stage in the future, sounds like another good book).

We are talking about **How to win when dealing with builders** throughout this book, but we need to be mindful that builders are people (believe it or not). So if we are able to look at ourselves and avoid certain painful situations, we are really learning **How to win when dealing with builders**, as well as learning how to deal with ourselves.

Correct?

Look, if you are planning to take on a heavy load, what do you think about? Me, I think about how I'm going to get from A to B in the easiest and safest way. This is called completing a **risk assessment** in relation to health and safety. We can liken this to moving bricks or taking on a new responsibility; the principles are still the same. (Again, this is in my opinion).

When you want a job doing by your ideal builder, think of what is required for that job to be done; put yourself

112

in the position of the builder. (Come on. Bear with me, I'll guide you through). As we have said, he or she is a person just like you and me. You don't have to be a qualified builder to determine an outcome. When I was an NVQ Assessor, I used to visualise what I needed to do to determine the candidate's competence. I used what's called a **storybook** approach. I visualised a beginning, middle, and an end. What I needed to ask myself was this; what were the tasks I needed to set out at the beginning? Was this task an achievable job for the candidate to achieve? Once the candidate was ready to be assessed, I would complete a visual or auditory assessment to deem competence. The result was a qualification.

I hope what I'm saying makes sense to you. If not let me know and I'll get Bruiser to try to explain it to you in a better way, which will be an experience for you, believe me!

It's just like writing a book; it has all three of these sections, generally speaking: a beginning, middle, and an ending. Remember old Bruiser before the bricks were dropped on his finger? What was he singing? That's right; I *did it my way* by old blue eyes himself, Frank Sinatra.

Bruiser had been moving bricks and materials for years and had never dropped a dozen bricks on his finger before. Guess what? He never did it again after that experience! Strange that, isn't it? He had to drop a dozen bricks on his finger to learn it wasn't something he was going to experience again, if he could help to prevent

113

it. The decision was made; that was the key I guess, the decision was made.

We are here to help guide you through the risk assessments of **How to win when dealing with builders** so you don't have to feel the pain of having a heavy load come down on you. The sad thing is most of you will still do things your way, even though you have this book, because you believe you know best. To be fair to you though, who am I to say you don't know best? All we are doing is giving you some suggestions on how you can **avoid pain and be happy**, in our opinion. The choice is then up to you.

Remember, if it makes sense why not try it? If it doesn't make sense to you, then you don't have to do it. This is a win-win situation, if you ask me. Some will say that no matter what we do, we can't lose! Well, actually, I must agree on that one. Do you?

Summary
- **Pay attention to what you are doing**
- **Don't get complacent**
- **Your way is not always the best way**
- **No pain, no gain**
- **Don't be hasty**
- **Avoidance is better than cure**
- **Do your risk assessment**
- **Evaluate the situation**

SECTION 11:
I couldn't lose!

There was a man who was a prisoner of war during the Second World War in a concentration camp called **Auschwitz**. He met another prisoner while he was there and became friends with him. I'm sure you are aware; concentration camps were places where very few people actually came out alive, especially from the notorious Auschwitz.

One of these special men had been separated from his wife and children during this time and the two friends made a pact that if they survived they would look up one another once the war was over. They promised that if they ever needed any help or support that they would do all they could to find the other person. They pledged their help and support to one other, hands were shaken, and home addresses were exchanged.

Time eventually passed and the war finally ended. The man who had been separated from his family found himself searching for them, and was in dire need of some help and support. For some reason, his old friend from the past who he had made a pact with in the concentration camp came to mind, so he found the address that he had kept in a safe place and set off with the hope of meeting up with his long lost friend.

Our friend finally arrived at the address given to him all those years earlier; with a little trepidation, he knocked

116

on the door not knowing what or who to find. When the door was opened and a younger version, it seemed, of his old friend stood in the doorway, our friend introduced himself, asked if his old friend still lived there, and if so would it be possible to speak with him. He was informed that his old friend had passed away the previous year. On hearing about the death of his old friend, the man could not withhold the emotion that suddenly overcame him and he burst into tears.

The young man at the door explained that he was the son of his old friend; he too was overcome with emotion. The son could feel the genuine love the stranger at the door had for his dead father.

Just as the man was about to thank the son for his time and be on his way, the son was impressed to ask how he knew his father and if he could help. This was an opportunity for the man to inform the son of his past friendship with his father and the ordeal they both had to endure in the concentration camp. On hearing this explanation, the son flung his arms around him and invited him in.

The son was able to inform his father's old friend that his father reminded him on his deathbed that if his old friend ever turned up and wanted assistance, help must be given. The son was so happy to be able to fulfil the dying wish of his father, by offering any help he possibly could. His father's friend informed the son that he was in need of a loan, so that he could resume his quest in finding his long lost wife and family. The son was happy to give the loan to our friend; off our

117

friend went, after promising to return and to pay back the loan.

Miraculously, it was about a year and a half later that the man finally found his long lost wife and family and was able to return to the son to repay the loan with interest. After the pleasantries were over, the man was able to ask a question that had been bothering him from the time he had left the son with the loan. "How is it that you were able to hand over the amount of money you did, to a comparatively complete stranger? I know I informed you of my relationship with your father, of our experiences and the promises we made to one another, but it still was an enormous amount of money to loan."

The son's reply was, "Well, I couldn't lose. You see if you returned with the loan and you paid me back the amount I gave you with the interest you insisted on paying, I would be a winner. And if you didn't come back and pay me the amount agreed, I was still a winner."

"OK, I'm confused", the man said. "What do you mean if I didn't return you would still be a winner?" To this, the son replied with a smile, "**I couldn't lose because I would be the wiser for the experience!**"

Wow. Now I don't know how you would view that under the same circumstances; I guess we shall, hopefully, never find out. But it would be a good idea to put safeguards in place just in case you are faced with a situation in the future where you may not get what you

118

expected in one form or another.

What me and Bruiser are trying to do is be able to give you some advice and guidance in all areas of your life, I suppose. We have learnt that in our working life and our social life the same problems seem to occur at times, which we need to overcome, and the principles on how to resolve those problems seem to be the same. Make sense? I don't know about you, but, just like Bruiser, when I've had something in life go wrong, I've definitely made a song and dance about it. I can sing and do have natural rhythm though. Not like Bruiser, mind; he can't sing or dance.

With a name like mine you wouldn't expect anything different though, would you? Remember my initials are **LB**, and no it's not lover boy, even though I've had my moments. I guess its human nature to try and find a way of hiding a problem so that it feels like it has gone away, when really all we are doing is prolonging the eventual agony.

When learning **How to win when dealing with builders**, you need to be careful how you put things to them, so that you and the builder don't assume anything other than what is expected. Remember when Bruiser was singing about doing it his way? Well, his way didn't work that day, did it? By doing things your own way when dealing with builders, your way may not be the right way. I guess doing things in our own way when dealing with people in general isn't always the right way either. So become **wiser**.

119

We suggest that you complete the required risk assessments. Did you know that most accidents on a building site are due to **slips and trips**? Always prepare the ground surface to take whatever is going to be placed on it. We know with hindsight that Bruiser would have taken more care before he placed those bricks on his finger. So now you've been warned, you have no more excuses!

My old mate Derek Day used to say that if you do something wrong once it can be classed as a mistake, but if you make the same mistake twice you deserve everything you get. Now that may sound harsh to some people, but he does have a point. Once Bruiser found comfort with the bucket of water he didn't want to remove it, because when he did the pain seemed to increase. All the water did was cool the affected area and numb the pain due to the coldness of the water. If he hadn't found the water to comfort him, he would have carried on until he found another solution for his problem.

Hey, guess what? You don't have to find the solution now on **How to win when dealing with builders**: we are giving you the solutions.

Good or what? Can we do an exercise together right now?

Come on, are you up for it? I need you to participate so that you get the full benefits; if you don't, I can definitely tell you that none of what I'm telling you will work. Why, because **action requires reaction in the form of a forward motion**!

120

We need to be together so here we go. I promise that this will not physically hurt you in any way whatsoever if you follow the instructions I'm going to give you. It will be better if we all **stand up! Come on, all stand up!** Excellent.

Now all I want you to do is raise your forefinger in the air for me. Please, do it now. OK, now hold your finger out in front of you at arm's length, with the tip of your finger pointing upwards. Now bring the tip of your finger and place it in the centre of your forehead. Why? **Because that is where you will find all of your life and building work answers; right there inside your head!**

Now please don't be offended by what I've just said to you, because I'm not trying to belittle you in any way. I honestly care about you becoming **happy** and successful without **pain** when learning **How to win when dealing with builders**, so please keep that in mind. You really do have the answers; it is just my job to have some fun with you and get you to believe in yourself along the way.

A good friend of mine once told me not to take life too seriously; I've found this to be true. All we have to do is learn from all of our mistakes and life experiences because that is what it's all about. How can you succeed if you haven't learnt to overcome some failures? Me and Bruiser are here to help you be more successful by giving you the tools to deal with any problem you may come across when dealing with builders.

121

In fact by the time we are finished with you, a build-er will not know that you haven't been in the build-ing game, in one form or another, during your lifetime. Trust me on this; we have a lot more information to share with you. You need to put the things you are taught into practice though, so you are able to gain a testimony for yourself. That is where the protection comes in for you.

OK, like I said, we all look for comfort when the results of our actions or the actions of someone else have caused us **pain**. When these problems come about, in our experience, it's down to people always seeing things in their own way. Once the problem arises and the lack of understanding kicks in with regards to the other party involved, the inevitable results are usually threats being made.

Look back at the incident with PC Nick Nick. If he had been aware of the problem Bruiser had in regards to his finger being raised in the air, do you think the re-sult, in the threats made to me and Bruiser, would have taken place? No! But then again, PC Nick Nick seemed to be on a vendetta; it was probably because Bruiser was better looking than he was.

During me and Bruiser's work experience, when going to court through misunderstandings or through threats being made, this could have been avoided in most cas-es. The problem is, once you go down the road of who's right and who's wrong, we usually go and ask people we know what they would do. We have found that if you ask enough people a question, eventually you will hear

122

the answer you want to hear.

This reminds me of the song *The Boxer* by Simon and Garfunkel. Still a man hears what he wants to hear and disregards the rest.

Please read that last statement over again and again until you get what I'm saying. If you understand what I'm saying, this one tip will save you a lot of money.

Listen to people who tell you what you *need* to hear and not what you want to hear!

We builders do get out the wrong side of the bed on occasions, as we all do. So stand back, re-evaluate the situation, look at the full picture; speak to people who will tell you what you **need** to hear. We are too hasty to make decisions at times, which can ultimately cause us **pain**. Who are the only people who never lose? These are solicitors when court comes into play. Besides, why make enemies? Sometimes winning the battle results in losing the war. Become **wiser**, and don't forget the story you have just read.

Try to learn something from any given situation and try not to repeat it if it causes pain. You have to make that decision. When we are in dispute we eventually have to sit down and find a solution. I know what you are thinking; there are people who will not listen to reason no matter what you do. Yes, I agree, and sometimes you will have to go down a legal path unfortunately. All I'm saying is just use all the tools me and Bruiser are giving you, and 99 times out of 100 you would have

123

avoided the painful situation or saved yourself from getting into the situation in the first place. If all else fails, you would have learnt something anyway, as we have just learnt from the story.

You are hopefully a lot **wiser** than when you started out. You have been given so much protection for the future. It's whether or not you see it and then use that information. Again, it's all part of the game of life we are all playing at the moment. Do me and Bruiser know everything? No, but we can give you the answers to what we have found works for us and then you decide what you do with those answers. Is everything 100% guaranteed? No? Well, actually some things are. We spoke about them earlier on in the book. I know that if you think about it, you can add to the guaranteed list on a daily basis as well.

Just look at all that rubbish me and Bruiser went through because he basically wasn't concentrating on what he was doing. No doubt Tweety Pie was taking up a lot of his thinking time and Bruiser has limited space for thinking at the best of times. I'm only joking, mate!

This triggered a knock-on effect of events that possibly could have been avoided. In the end, it all worked out for good, but there will be times when things will not work out the way we hoped for if we are not careful.

So, remember to be careful where you are putting your fingers and where you point your finger. If you are pointing at yourself you are probably doing things right. Think about that! After all, when it comes down

124

to it, we only have ourselves to blame really, don't we? But it's much easier to blame someone else!

Summary
- **Make friends**
- **You never know when you will need a friend**
- **Speak to the right people**
- **Become wiser**
- **Learn the game of life**
- **Point at yourself**
- **Take responsibility**

125

How to win when dealing with builders

SECTION 12:
Wannabe Kev known as Bev

Now this is the story of Wannabe Kev known as Bev. Some would call him a snake in the grass, for want of a better word. Actually, there are plenty of better words to describe him, but let's leave it at that. We are not wishing to infer that women are not great people because we know that behind every good man there will be found a better woman. Fact! The reason we call him Bev is because it's just a term we use in the building game; when a man doesn't do what men should do, we say they should have been a women. All he needed was a dress and he could have been mistaken for a woman anyway. He would have been a very ugly woman though! So we shall call him Bev, if that's OK.

Me and Bruiser came across Bev some time ago now. Bruiser was able to sum him up in two words, a spineless dick. He was a typical **wannabe** at all costs rich and successful person, and would stitch you up if he was smart enough to do so. He is typical of someone who hasn't got a clue what it's like to work on a building site, comes in to revolutionise our industry, but gives it a bad name.

His favourite pastime is going out on his racing bike, kitted out in his all-in-one Lycra outfit pretending he's in the *Tour de France*. At the weekend he would play in a boy band where he was a wannabe pop star. You've got it; all in one Elvis suit, a chain hanging from his neck,

127

sovereign rings on each finger. In fact, a sleazy character whose minder is his wife.

We call her The Witch. Any problems Bev has, he calls on her to stick up for him and fight his battles because he hasn't got the bottle to do his own dirty work. The Witch's favourite day off in the year is Halloween, where she goes for a flight on her broomstick.

If a man confronts Bev he cowers in a corner and lies, saying, "Please don't hurt me because I was picked on by girls at school!" On one occasion, me and Bruiser were about to complete some work for him and Bruiser wasn't happy because Bev tried to get him to start a job that he wasn't able to do, because he hadn't been given the correct training. Now Bev tried to verbally bully Bruiser into completing the job, because all he cared about was getting paid from the Government when a candidate was successfully assessed and confirmed competent. Now Bruiser informed him that this would not be legal, due to the fact that he hadn't received the required training to assess the candidates, and under health and safety regulations this would put Bruiser and the candidates at risk.

Bev didn't care that Bruiser hadn't received the correct training, even though there were possible underground cables involved in the assessment criteria and without the required training this would be another reason not to put anyone at risk. Now Bev, being a lowlife, didn't care about the situation and threatened Bruiser with having to face The Witch in a disciplinary situation. Bruiser doesn't take kindly to being threat-

128

ened, as I've said, so he informed Bev not to threaten him. Well Bev wouldn't listen to him so a quiet word from Bruiser was given in Bev's ear; the rest is history. Yes, Bev landed up in the corner of his office, thumb in his mouth, calling out to The Witch for help.

The Witch informed me and Bruiser that our services were no longer required. Now Bev has been given a false sense of security, because little does he know that, at the right time, me and Bruiser are going to send him a present with a thank you note attached to it. (Yes, I know you shall be reading this, Bev). The present is going to be well presented, because we feel Bev is a deserving candidate for the present.

You don't have to use threats or violence to get rid of people like Bev. What hurts them most is when their god is affected, their god being money.

We shall inform you at a later date how we got on. It will be funny!

So a word of advice to all you wannabe Bevs who are causing our industry to have a bad name: Me and Bruiser know who you are and we are going to help clean up our industry in providing safe working environments through correct training for people. We shall do all we can to get rid of lowlifes like Bev.

There are numerous injuries caused to workers due to the wannabe Bevs of our industry, but, unfortunately, we have found that the system is not weeding them out as they should. Well, me and Bruiser will do our best to change this. Peacefully, I might add. Come the revolution, no doubt we shall see you all up against the wall with us.

Sorry about that, but we want to protect people from lowlifes if possible. We do know how difficult it is at times when dealing with some builders. That's why me and Bruiser will be striving to help and protect people like you as much as we can, and show you **How to win when dealing with builders**.

Be careful of the Bevs of our industry. They come in sheep's clothing (in Kev known as Bev's case coward's clothing) and will not hesitate in dropping you in it.

Take a look in the section Building works' requirements, because this section will also be of help to you. It's so frustrating when we hear about the cowboy builders who have galloped off on their horses again, after robbing someone's bank account. It is especially frustrating when there is helpful information within the system that people are not aware of. Well, that's the reason for writing this book, so that you now have the resources necessary to know **How to win when dealing with builders**.

I thank the Government for the information on their website, because it's made freely available to all, so take a look.

130

Summary

- **Be careful**
- **Say no to unsafe practices**
- **You have been given the knowledge**
- **Get information from creditable sources**

How to win when dealing with builders

SECTION 13:
Building work requirements

We've included the following sections because we feel there is a wealth of information provided for you by this Government site. We have copied a great deal of the information so that you have a source ready at hand. It is not copied word for word in all places, so please check on the site below. Me and Bruiser are not legal experts. We strongly recommend that when you read any information you seek professional advice and guidance before making any monetary or legally binding decisions. To find the information provided it can be found at www.direct.gov.uk (go to the 'Home and community' section). The copyright belongs to the Crown.

What is planning permission?
When it comes to building projects, me and Bruiser have seen some nightmare situations where people have gone ahead and completed work without the proper authority. We are going to go over some areas that we feel you need to be aware of.

So, what does planning permission actually mean?

This means that you ask your local planning author-ity if you can go ahead and do a certain type of work. When permission has been granted by the authority they will normally have been in contact with you and

133

stipulated what is required from you before you would have received the go ahead.

It is **your** responsibility to get planning permission.

As I said, you apply to your planning authority. Where smaller jobs are concerned, there are many times when you don't need planning permission, on private houses as an example. They call these **Permitted Developments**. These developments still have to follow certain building rules though.

When I built my own extension, I applied to the local planning authority for a document known as a Lawful Development Certificate. This means that I was granted building work permission.

How planning permission works

Your local council has the responsibility in deciding what can be developed in your area. This can be anything from a new shopping centre to an extension to a house, as was the case in my situation.

When it comes to certain jobs, planning permission is not always needed, as long as certain limits or conditions are met.

But always check.

Bigger projects like shops and supermarkets always require planning permission.

134

Before you apply for planning permission

A planning application can be a complex process and you need to have several documents ready before you can complete the application form.

You need to make sure you have the necessary plans and mandatory national and local documents in place.

Example:

You always need a site location plan that shows where the proposed development is in relation to other properties in the area. You also need a block plan, which shows the proposed development in relation to the property boundary.

Check with your local planning officer and you will be informed what documents are required.

If you don't want to apply for planning permission yourself

If you don't want the aggro of handling the application yourself, you can ask your architect, solicitor, agent, or builder to do it for you.

If you are not the sole owner of the property or the property is leasehold you need to inform the owner/part owner and any leaseholders who have at least seven years left on their lease.

The planning application is a process

Learn the process.

The local planning authority will check the planning application and make it public so that it gives other people the opportunity to comment if they want to. Once this is completed, the council will decide if your application is granted or declined.

Never start the building operation until you have the planning agreed and approved: you will receive written confirmation.

If your planning application is refused you need to ask the planning department why this is the case. You may have to make an amendment to the application and send it in again. If all else fails and you think the local authority is being unreasonable, you have the right of appealing to the Secretary of State.

The council will normally decide your application within eight weeks. If it requires longer, you shall be informed in writing for an extension period. This happens when the project is complex or when it's going to affect a lot of people.

When planning permission is granted

By law, any planning permission expires after a certain period.

Make sure you ask how to extend the permission and other consents you need before any building work is

136

started. Always ask for advice and guidance from the department. Sometimes an application is granted with conditions attached to it: the authority has to give the reasons for the conditions.

What me and Bruiser are trying to do is give you the required education you need to protect yourself. You may think that you don't need to know all this because there is no way you are going to do this work yourself. Well that's great, if that's what you want.

Remember: Ignorance is bliss until it catches up with you!

There is a saying, **Better the devil you know**. That way you are not going to have some pain to deal with along the way.

Building regulations
Again, it's your responsibility as the owner of the property (or land) in question.

It's ultimately your responsibility to comply with the relevant planning rules and building regulations (regardless of the need to apply for planning permission and/or restoration).

Always discuss with your local authority what is required **before** work is commenced.

Me and Bruiser have been on jobs where work has been taken down or had to be restored back to the original

137

standard. This can cost a fortune, so don't give these people the hump or you will definitely face the consequences. Trust me. Do not risk it!

The responsibility of the building work is with the person who is carrying out the work. If they are not the same person, it's the owner of the property.

Before you start work

Check with your local authority to see if there are any other charges you are likely to have to pay. There can be other levies you may be required to pay, so check these out with your local authority. One of these levies came about on 6th April 2010 through the **community infrastructure levy**. A development may be liable for a charge under the community infrastructure levy (CIL) if the local authority planning department has chosen to set a charge in its area, for instance.

We don't want to go into all the different things the authorities may be doing in this guide, but do your checks to find out if there are other taxes you will have to pay. Basically, me and Bruiser see it as another way of getting money from us.

Building regulations apply both here in England and in Wales and are there to promote standards for most aspects of a building construction. Building regulations are statutory instruments that seek to ensure that the policies set out in the relevant legislation are carried out. Building regulations' approval is required for most building work in the UK. Building regulations that ap-

138

ply across England and Wales are set out in the Building Act 1984 while those that apply across Scotland are set out in the Building (Scotland) Act 2003.

The UK Government is responsible for the relevant legislation and administration in England and Wales, the Scottish Government is responsible for the issue in Scotland, and the Northern Ireland Executive has responsibility within its jurisdiction. These aspects include energy efficiency in buildings, the needs of people with disabilities, and the needs of people in accessing and moving around buildings.

Again, speak to the building department of your local authority to ask what is required in relation to the relevant documents.

How to get approval

Building regulations apply to most building work, so it's important that you know when approval is needed.

The building control bodies (BCBs) have the responsibility to check that the building regulations have been met.

This is through the private sector as an approved inspector or from the local authority. The person who is carrying out the work has the option of who to go through.

How to get the approval depends on which of these two bodies are used.

139

The approval process

If you go through the local authority route, the procedures are set out in the building regulations. Some procedures relate to when work is being done; other procedures relate to pre site procedures.

On site approval

Once the work is underway, there are regular on site visits by the building inspector, who is part of the building control service. He visits the work while in progression to make sure that the building regulation requirements are adhered to.

Pre- site approval

If you choose the local authority building control service, there are three types of application for approval you can make.

1. A building notice

You don't need plans for this process so it's much quicker than the 'full plans' application.

If you use this procedure, you need to make sure that you are confident that the work will definitely comply with the buildings regulations or you will risk having to put the work right if it doesn't, if the local authority requests it. This means that you don't have the protection you would if you had 'full plans' approval.

Once you have informed your local authority and you have given your 'building notice' in to them, and you

140

have informed them that you are ready to start, the work will then be inspected as work progresses. The inspector will inform you if the work doesn't comply with the building regulations, so that the work can be rectified.

A *building notice* is valid for three years from the date the notice was deposited to the local authority. It will lapse if the building work isn't started.

A completion certificate is not required by the local authority under the building notice procedure. Because no full plans are produced it's not possible to ask for a determination if your local authority tells you your work doesn't comply with the building regulations.

2. Full plans

If you submit full plans you can apply for building regulations' approval from your local building control service.

When you put in an application under this procedure, there needs to be plans and other information showing all construction details. This should ideally be done well in advance of the building work start date. Once the plans are checked by the local authority they will consult with any other appropriate authorities such as sewerage and fire, as an example.

This procedure must take place within five weeks and the local authority will be issuing you with a decision, or, if you agree, up to two months from when the application was submitted. If the plans comply with the

141

building regulations a notice of approval will be issued to you. If the local authority isn't happy with the plans you may be asked to make amendments or provide more detail. You could be issued with a conditional approval. This will specify that further plans need to be submitted or there will need to be a modification to the plans.

The local authority can only apply conditions if you have asked them to do so or have given your consent. A condition or consent must be made in writing.

A full plans approval notice is valid for three years from the date the plans were deposited. Once the three years have expired, the local authority may send you a notice to declare the approval has no effect if the building work is not commenced.

Again, the local authority representative will carry out regular inspections once the work is in progress. At various stages in the inspection process, the local authority inspector will come out to check that the building regulations are adhered to. The inspections will take place at the foundation stage, drainage inspection, and at damp proof course stage, as examples. A full stage procedure inspection information document would be supplied prior to operations taking place. Always check and ask for advice and guidance when dealing with your local authority.

If you request a completion certificate to be issued by the local authority one will be provided as long as the building regulations have been complied with.

142

With the full plans procedure, if a disagreement arises within the local authority it enables you to ask for a 'determination' from the Department for Communities and Local Government (in England) or (in Wales) the Welsh Assembly about whether your plans do or do not comply with the building regulations.

3. Regularisation

Where works are being done without building regulations' approval, the owner may be prosecuted. However, to facilitate people to have work approval, there is a process called regularisation.

A regularisation application is a retrospective application relating to previously authorised works, i.e. works carried out without building regulations' consent, started on or after 11th November 1985.The purpose of this procedure is to regulate the unauthorised work and obtain a certificate of regularisation.

Depending on the exposure, circumstances, removal and/or rectification of works it may be necessary to establish compliance with the building regulations.

Again, check with your local authority building control service to discuss your individual circumstances before submitting a regularisation application.

Finding an Electrician

It's been estimated that about 6,700 fires a year are reported as having an electrical source, which includes faulty or inadequate wiring.

The fires, along with the shock accidents, cause around 43 fatalities and 2,900 serious injuries every year.

Cables, switches, socket-outlets and other equipment can get worn over time and so it's important to get them checked and replaced by a qualified electrician.

You can find out more about the organisations that approve electricians and search for a qualified tradesman on the Electrical Safety Council's website www.esc.org.uk

Electrician registration scheme organisations

It is so important that electrical work is carried out only by those with the necessary knowledge, skill, and experience of the type of electrical work to be undertaken.

The following organisations run the registration schemes for competent electricians (these are sometimes called 'competent person' schemes):

- BRE certification
- British standards institute (BS)
- ELECSA
- The National Association of Professional Inspectors and Testers (NAPIT)
- NICEIC certification services

These schemes ensure that traders who sign up are fully qualified to do electrical work and provide a complaints procedure.
You may also need to use a competent person to comply with building regulations.

144

Finding a Plumber

If you are considering employing a plumber to carry out work in your home, it is important to make sure they are competent, reliable, trustworthy, and professional.

Recommendations

The Institute of Plumbing and Heating Engineering (IPHE), which is the professional body for the plumbing industry, recommends that when finding a plumber you should:

- Ask friends/relatives/neighbours who they use.
- Use a member of the Institute of Plumbing and Heating Engineering – members have to hold recognised qualifications in plumbing and/or extensive experience.
- Get at least three quotes and when asking for quotes find out if there is a call out fee, how many people will be doing the job, and if the price per hour includes all the workmen/women or if more is charged per plumber.
- Ask for a written quote – unless there are unforeseen costs, the final bill should not deviate too far from this initial written quote.
- Clearly explain all of the work you need doing – write it all down if possible.
- Ask how long the job will take.

When you have found a plumber and the job is completed, ask for a full breakdown of the bill so you know where your money has gone.

145

Gas safety at home

A poorly maintained gas appliance can cause carbon monoxide poisoning. Learn more about the symptoms of this and how to prevent it. Find out what your rights and responsibilities for gas safety are as a tenant, landlord, or homeowner.

Gas Safe Register

Gas Safe Register replaced Corgi as the organisation responsible for gas safety in Great Britain in 2009.

To find a gas safe registered engineer, visit the Gas Safe Register website www.gassaferegister.co.uk or call 0800 408 5500.

Summary

- What is planning permission?
- How planning permission works
- Before you apply for planning permission
- If you don't want to apply for planning permission
- The planning application is a process
- When planning permission is granted
- Building regulations
- Before you start work
- How to get approval
- The approval process
- On site approval
- Pre site approval
- A building notice
- Full plans
- Regularisation
- Finding an electrician
- Electrician Registration Schemes
- Finding a plumber
- Recommendations
- Gas safety at home
- Gas Safety Register

How to win when dealing with builders

SECTION 14:
Dick Dastardly and Muttley

"Bruiser, is there anything that comes to mind in relation to what we can share, from your inspired memory bank? You have been sleeping for the past four hours and, as you told me before, this is your inspiration time. So what inspiration do you have to offer?"

Bruiser's reply: "Dick Dastardly and Muttley!"

"Dick Dastardly and Muttley? What are you talking about? Are you going Wacky or what?"

Bruiser never ceases to amaze me; his memory for cartoon characters makes me laugh. Bruiser has always kept the child within, which he won't let go of. There's probably something for all of us to learn from that.

Bruiser always amazes me on how he turns previous experiences into positive outcomes, through funny memories he has stored in his mind over the years. Let me give you some background information as to who Dick Dastardly and Muttley are. *Wacky Races* is an animated television series produced by Hanna-Barbera, which ran in the late 60s. The series features eleven different cars racing against each other in various rallies throughout North America, each driver hoping to win the title of the World's Wackiest Racer. Two of those characters are Dick Dastardly and Muttley in the mean machine 00. They were the villains of the series who

149

drove a purple rocket-powered car with an abundance of concealed weapons and the ability to fly. Muttley is his wheezily, snickering anthropomorphic dog hench-man. Dastardly concocts plans and traps in order to maintain a lead, but most of his plans backfire, causing him to finish in last place[6].

Now picture this. Dick Dastardly and Muttley are prob-ably related to spineless Kev known as Bev, come to think about it. Me and Bruiser came across these two due to us hearing about a scam they had pulled on an elderly couple. Once again, the vulnerable and gullible were the victims of these two lowlife characters. They were able to persuade the couple to part with £2,000 up front so that they were able to begin a conversion to the old couple's property. The couple were fooled by the business cards and headed paper that looked very professional, but had no real substance if the couple had done their due diligence.

The couple should have checked to see if they were members of the professional body they said they were members of, and they would have found that they had been blacklisted. If they had completed a credit check on Dick Dastardly and Muttley they would also have found that they had a nightmare credit history. If they had followed up on the references they were given, they would have found that the addresses given were bogus. The list goes on.

The Gruesome Twosome, as we've now named Dick and

---

6 More detailed information can be found on the Wikipedia free encyclopaedia site under 'Wacky Races' who own the copyright.

Muttley, would always start the race hoping to win by cleaning out people's bank balances. (The Gruesome Twosome, by the way, is another couple of characters from *Wacky Races*). They have the getaway vehicle in place in the form of no fixed company address to begin with. (Always check out the company address when dealing with builders).

These two always deal with job valuations over a certain amount of money; in this case, they had estimated £40,000. They started off by removing walls and using construction props that were highly unsafe. They built partial block walling and used the old timber base structure as a foundation to build the block walls on. They also left the rear of the property exposed to outside elements.

The concealed weapons I referred to earlier was the threat that if more money wasn't given they were unable to continue the work. So the old couple handed over more money expecting the work to be continued. Remember, if the work being achieved by the builder is slow you may think that this is normal but it is not always the case.

Again, this is where the contract you have with the builder comes into play. There should be a stage completion date clause written into the contract, so that any interim payments that have been agreed are dependent on completion of the tasks stipulated in the agreement.

Unfortunately the contract that was agreed with the

151

couple had no reference to this and the vulnerable couple just relied on trusting the Gruesome Twosome. Now it wasn't the first time they had pulled this scam and the word always gets around about what they are doing. They are the type who always brags about what they are up to, usually in the pub after a lot of alcohol has been consumed. They have had their just rewards in a number of ways, which you don't need to know about (nothing to do with me and Bruiser, mind).

The Gruesome Twosome never finishes the race, because they get too greedy. Unfortunately, prior to this happening, the victims have to pay the price.

In *Wacky Races*, Dick Dastardly and Muttley, or the Gruesome Twosome as we call them, always try to cut corners or get something for nothing at someone's expense. Now after a long process in having to undo what they had done, me and Bruiser were able to go and put the work right. But it was a painful lesson for our vulnerable old couple to have to learn. The good news is you don't have to experience the Gruesome Twosome. You are receiving so much protection now; there is really no need for you not to succeed. You are being taught **How to win when dealing with builders**, and the armour you are being given is invaluable. But it's only a protection if you use it correctly.

It's important that you imagine yourself in the same situation after reading these stories, because you are less likely to allow yourself to be conned. Someone once said to me, "The hardest thing about running is watching someone else!" What he was referring to is,

152

when he watched what the people were going through he called it the pain to gain process when they are running to get fit, he felt so happy that he wasn't going through that pain. **You don't have to go through the pain to gain process.** We don't want to see that.

So again, go over what you have just been reading and put yourself in the old couple's situation. Think about what you will do differently from now on if you come across the Gruesome Twosome further on down the road.

You make that decision now! It's so powerful.

Summary
- **Be careful of money demanded up front**
- **Check builders' creditability**
- **Contract clauses**
- **Protect yourself**

How to win when dealing with builders

SECTION 15:
Billy Bone Idol

This section will give you an excellent understanding of terminology and language where building materials and tools are concerned. If you have some general knowledge in relation to the terms you are going to come across when speaking to builders you will be onto a winner.

Me and Bruiser have found that when you can have a discussion with someone about their field of work it gives you more credibility when dealing with them. A great deal of the terms you hear will be alien to you, so we want to teach you these terms that will give you more armour, metaphorically speaking.

Before we go on, I just want to ask Bruiser's opinion on the best route for us to go down, if that's OK.

"Bruiser, what in your opinion is the best way to teach our extended family (that's you, by the way) about the terms we use, so it can be a protection for them?"

"Tell them about your six month apprentice Billy Bone Idol."

OK, now this was an experience I shall never forget. Me and Bruiser have learnt to steer clear of getting involved with people who bring too much baggage (meaning in this case life history/problems) when working with them every day, because if you are not careful they will be passing that baggage onto you.

Me and Bruiser had come across a roofer who we called Jake the Slate. Don't ask me why we like calling people by their nicknames. I don't know where it came from to be honest; it's just something we've always done. It's probably because it is easier for us to remember the person concerned. Now, when we were working on a certain job, Jake the Slate got talking to me and persuaded me to assess his son to see if he had the makings of a bricklayer.

I was obviously having one of those head in the cloud days, when most of what I said to people was "yes" without thinking. Normally I would think twice about taking on certain commitments, but on that particular day Jake the Slate did a charm job on me, I believe.

I landed up working with Jake the Slate's son, Billy. I decided to work with his son because Bruiser was going to be supervising on another job, so I got conned into dealing with young Billy boy. Let me give you a little background in relation to Billy. Billy's dad informed me that his son had been a naughty boy at some stage in his young life, because he had served a term in Her Majesty's borstal and had some scars to prove it. When I got to know Billy, he showed me some horrendous scars over both of his knees and down part of his shins, which needed skin grafts.

Apparently Billy had been given a job to do whilst he

156

was training in borstal, where he had to level out a load of concrete that had been poured out over a given area. Billy's dad informed me that Billy's supervisor on the day of the incident was teaching a group of lads including Billy how to level a load of concrete. Billy called the procedure **dragging**, which meant getting the concrete level. Apparently Billy decided to kneel down whilst he was dragging the concrete, because it was a lot easier than standing up. Anyway, according to Billy, the supervisor didn't inform him that it was dangerous to kneel in concrete due to the lime/cement, which is part of the ingredients within the concrete.

Billy said that he wasn't aware of anything going on underneath his trousers where his knees were, due to the numbing effect the cold concrete had on his knees. When he finally got up from his knees after spending a considerable amount of time on them, he happened to see a large area of red on both knees, which showed visibly on the outside of his trousers. When he inspected his knees he realised that he had serious burns on both of them due to the effect of the lime.

When I saw the condition of his legs I felt sorry for him, to be honest. I again learnt how important it is to be educated in areas of health and safety when working with building materials, because most materials can be hazardous in one way or another: you need to be aware of the dangers. You also need to make sure that when builders are doing work for you they are following health and safety procedures. I shall be going over some areas of health and safety with you later.

Again, that old saying comes to mind: **"Ignorance is bliss until it catches up with you!"**

Billy had a lot of the muscle tissue from behind his knee area removed due to the severe burns he had received and he had to have skin grafts. I don't know all of the facts but I know enough to be able to say that you need to be aware of the correct personal protective clothing to wear when working with building materials. Don't forget what you've learnt already: **never assume anything**; we're giving you the knowledge. The reason I'm being more graphic in relation to this serious problem happening to Billy is because it gives you some idea how harmful some building materials can be. If cement/lime dust is breathed into our lungs this can also cause serious problems over time: that is why the correct face masks and eye protection is so important.

I shall leave it there in relation to what happened to Billy and the hazards you can come up against and go onto when I first was introduced to him by his dad, Jake the Slate. Billy wasn't a big lad; he was quite small and skinny and looked like he needed a size eight boot up his posterior, to be honest. You know what I mean, don't you? He just didn't seem to have any get up and go about him; in fact, he seemed to have an attitude problem. When Jake the Slate asked me to assess Billy to see if, in my opinion, he was up for working as a bricklayer, I thought "is Jake having a laugh or what? Is this a wind up?"

Well, after the introduction and when Jake the Slate finally left Billy with me, I was about to find out for

158

myself what Billy's mind set was like. As soon as Jake the Slate had got into his car and was out of sight, Billy went over to the empty wheelbarrow that was close by and sat in it with his legs dangling over the sides, laid back as if he was in a bed. I knew there and then that the gauntlet had been laid down by Billy to see if I was up for the challenge. Normally I think to myself, I can do without the aggro, but I suppose I saw something in Billy I liked so I was ready to see what he was made of. I asked him what he wanted to do whilst he was with me. His reply: "As little as possible!"

My response was that if he thought that this was going to happen he needs to think again. I informed him that if he was going to be working with me he would need to change his mind set from the start otherwise we might as well part company now. If he didn't get out of the wheelbarrow, me and him were going to fall out; in fact he would be literally falling out of the wheelbarrow head first.

Now I believe that Billy wasn't as stupid as he looked, because he quickly got out of the wheelbarrow as I moved forward. "What! How you could be so mean?" some of you might be saying. "You can't do that in this day and age!" I bet some of you are thinking, "What? A poor young lad being frightened by a good looking builder like him? That is brutal!" When I first started in the building industry I can tell you stories that would make your hair curl and your toes curl for that matter. There have been far worse things that have happened to me! How Billy responded to me, and seeing what he was going to do, was a way of me knowing if I needed to call Jake the Slate to come and take Billy back or if I could do something with him. Well, he passed his first test; it was called **showing some respect**.

You may think it was showing fear, but either way it worked. I've told you before; it's all a game and this was a technique that has been used on most of us in the building game over the years, in one form or another. My next question to him was "What do you really want to become? What is your ideal profession, Billy?" Well, I did ask, so who am I to say it can't happen. Billy's answer was to become a Pop Idol! A new nickname was created out of thin air that day, Billy Bone Idol. Billy's new name summed him up quite nicely, even if I do say so myself. So, my initial findings were that I was dealing with a self-confessed lazy person and if I could teach him how to become a Pop Idol I was on to a winner. Come to think about it, Billy Bone Idol was on his way to becoming a Pop Idol with the lack of qualities he was showing. To you budding pop stars, I'm only joking.

Was Billy Bone Idol mastermind potential? My initial assessment was completed and my next assessment was to see what he actually knew about brickwork terms used within the building industry. I decided to set him some questions, for him to take away, fill in the answers, and bring back to me in a couple of days' time. I wanted to know if he was able to show some initiative and go away and do some research to find the answers. At least it would give me some idea of what work was needed to get him on the first steps to becoming a bricklayer.

160

The questions were given to him at the end of the working day. Billy promised he would answer all of the questions and bring them back to me in a couple of days. I said to him that he needed to find the answers himself, because I shall ask him the same questions verbally to test his knowledge, which he agreed to do. Let me share with you the 30 questions I gave him and give you the correct answers.

This is an opportunity for you to learn these terms for your own protection, for future reference. Don't forget, if you are forewarned you are forearmed when learning **How to win when dealing with builders**.

Billy was given a couple of days to find the answers to these questions, but, to be honest, he could have easily completed the task in less than a day by looking on the internet or looking the terms up in library books.

Questions and Answers: Bricklaying Terms

1. What is a bat?

Answer: a cut brick. A quarter-bat is one quarter the length of a stretcher. A half-bat is one half.

2. What is a closer?

Answer: a cut brick commonly known as a quarter-bat, which is used to change the bond at quoins (Quoins are the corner of a wall in this case).

3. What are ties?

Answer: ties or cavity ties are used to tie layers of brickwork into one another, to form a structural whole.

4. What is a shiner?

Answer: a brick laid on the long narrow side with the broad side exposed.

5. What is a snapped header?

Answer: a half-bat laid to appear as a header; commonly used to build short-radii half brick walls or decorative features.

6. What is a squint?

Answer: a brick that is specially made to bond around external quoins of obtuse angles; typically 60 or 45 degrees.

7. What is a dog leg?

Answer: a brick that is specially made to bond around internal acute angles; typically 60 or 45 degrees.

8. What is a voussoir?

Answer: a supporting brick in an arch usually shaped to ensure that the joints appear even.

9. What is a spot board?

Answer: a flat square board where mortar is placed.

10. What is a cramp?

Answer: a tie used to secure a window or door frame.

11. What is a movement joint?

Answer: a straight joint formed in a wall to contain compressible material, in order to prevent cracking as the wall contracts or expands.

162

12. What is an air brick?

Answer: a brick with perforations to allow the passage of air through a wall; usually used to permit the ventilation of under floor areas.

13. What is a pier?

Answer: a freestanding section of masonry, such as a pillar or panel.

14. What is a quoin?

Answer: a corner in masonry.

15. What is a dog tooth?

Answer: a course of headers where alternate bricks project from the face.

16. What is a sleeper wall?

Answer: a low wall whose function is to provide support, typically to floor joists.

17. What is a saw tooth?

Answer: a course of headers laid at a 45 degree angle to the main face.

18. What is a honeycombed wall?

Answer: a wall, usually stretcher bond, in which the vertical joints are opened up to the size of a quarter-bat to allow air to circulate. Commonly used in sleeper walls.

19. What is a party wall?

Answer: a wall shared by two properties.

20. What is a firewall?

Answer: a wall specifically constructed to compart-mentalise a building in order to prevent fire spread.

21. What is toothing?

Answer: the forming of a temporary stopped end in such a way as to allow the bond to continue at a later date as the work proceeds.

22. What is tumbling in?

Answer: bonding a battered buttress or breast into a horizontal wall.

23. What is racking back?

Answer: stepping back the bond as the wall increases in height in order to allow the work to proceed at a future date.

24. What is a bullnose?

Answer: a round edged brick that is useful for window sills, on low and free standing walls.

25. What is a stretcher?

Answer: a brick laid horizontally flat, with the long side of the brick exposed on the outer face of the wall.

26. What is a bond?

Answer: a pattern in which bricks are laid.

27. What is a header?

Answer: a brick laid flat with the short end of the brick exposed.

28. What is a soldier?

Answer: a brick laid vertically with the narrow ('stretch-er') side exposed.

164

29. What is a sailor?

Answer: a brick laid vertically with the broad side exposed.

30. What is a frog?

Answer: a frog is a recessed part of a surface of a brick.

Now Billy Bone Idol contacted me three days later with the excuse he lost the questions I gave him and informed me that he finally managed to find them yesterday. He said he had been up most of the night doing his research because he didn't want to let me down. Do you know what I thought when he told me this? I thought, bless his little heart, he really cares about me! If you believe that you will also believe that one day Bruiser will become a ballet dancer. What a thought. So the questions were handed back to me with the answers he had come up with. Here they are, for you to decide if Billy Bone Idol was worthy of the award for the Brain of Britain.

Billy's answers to the question paper

1. What is a bat?

Answer: a vampire's pet bird.

2. What is a closer?

Answer: when you finish having an argument with someone, you have to put a closer to it.

3. What are ties?

Answer: clothing you wear around your neck.

4. What is a shiner?

Answer: this is bruising around your eye when you get punched in it.

5. What is a snapped header?

Answer: when you lay the 'nut' (he means head butt) on someone quickly.

6 What is a squint?

Answer: when the sun shines in your eyes.

7. What is a dog leg?

Answer: stupid question! They have four of them!

8. What is a voussoir?

Answer: a place where French women go.

9. What is a spot board?

 Answer: a board used for picking zits. (zits are spots and spots are acne).

10. What is a cramp?

Answer: you get it in your leg when you play football. It kills!

11. What is a movement joint?

Answer: when you pass around a spliff around at a party.

12. What is an air brick?

Answer: a brick you throw through the air.

13. What is a pier?

Answer: you find them at the seaside near the sea.

14. What is a quoin?

166

Answer: it's money.

15. What is a dog tooth?

Answer: you find it in a dog's mouth.

16. What is a sleeper wall?

Answer: a wall you sleep up against when you're tired.

17. What is a saw tooth?

Answer: when your tooth hurts.

18. What is a honeycombed wall?

Answer: I think it's found in a bee's nest.

19. What is a party wall?

Answer: this is found in a room where you are having a party.

20. What is a firewall?

Answer: a wall that's on fire.

21. What is toothing?

Answer: I've had this question before. You find them in your mouth.

22. What is tumbling in?

Answer: when there's a fight and everyone joins in.

23. What is racking back?

Answer: using a garden rake, for instance.

24. What is a bullnose?

Answer: you find it on a bull's face.

25. What is a stretcher?

Answer: something you lay on and are taken to hospital on if you upset 'Bruiser'.

26. What is a bond?

Answer: surname of James 007.

27. What is a header?

Answer: when you head a football.

28. What is a soldier?

Answer: someone who's in the army.

29. What is a sailor?

Answer: someone who's in the navy.

30. What is a frog?

Answer: a thing that you find in water and can jump.

Now, am I missing something here or do you think he was having a laugh? Well, I found out after questioning him that he wasn't having a laugh; he was serious! Now in all the years I've been dealing with people, I think I'm going to put Billy Bone Idol up there with the best of them, for being original with the answers he gave. For a few minutes when I started reading them, I thought I was on another planet. Actually I wanted to be on another planet, come to think about it.

By the way, how would you do if I was to set you a test now on what you have learnt? One of the questions might be have you actually learnt something by what you have been reading?

168

Hopefully the answer would be "yes". Just like Billy Bone Idol we all have to make choices and come up with the answers at some stage, whether we get them right or not. Billy made excuses to himself first before making them to me, especially when it came to not giving me the question paper as agreed. Do we all do that sometimes? I know I do, make an excuse that is.

For instance, computers aren't my thing really, so I would make excuses why I couldn't do something on them at times. This was because I didn't find them easy to use, because I don't enjoy technical things; this was mainly due to my limited knowledge within this area. I now look forward to getting on the computer so that I can start writing again. It's all about finding the **passion** to do something and then it becomes easier, I've found. After speaking to Billy Bone Idol about the answers he gave, he was still in denial and blamed the internet for giving him the answers.

I had to think about this for a while before I was able to come up with a plausible reason for him to make that statement. Here is what I came up with.

1. I gave Billy the questions after I had explained the reason for me giving them to him and he agreed that he would complete them.

2. I gave him the questions because I wanted to test his desire to learn.

3. I also gave him the questions because I thought that if he couldn't be bothered to look for the answers I would be wasting my time with him.

With the above reasons I have just given, I believed I had good reason to give up on him because, in my opinion, he failed in answering all of the questions correctly.

Then I thought, "**What if** he didn't really understand the reason for me giving the questions, even though he agreed to complete them? **What if** he had the desire to learn, but wasn't all that good in finding the answers? **What if** he was bothered and he completed all of the questions and gave them to me knowing that they were probably the answers I wasn't looking for? At least he gave the correct answers to questions in relation to another subject matter".

I hope this is making sense. You see, after some investigation, I found out that Billy was a little dyslexic and had been given some help in writing the answers down. I also learnt that he had low self-esteem. What a difference it makes when we say **what if** at times and look at things in a different way.

Me and Bruiser are hoping that you are seeing things in a different way and are getting to understand the reason we are giving you these stories to consider. We understand things better by stories and we are hoping you do too. Hopefully, when you keep reading these stories they will be embedded in your subconscious. Look for the reason **why** you would benefit from understanding the terms we've just discussed. Think about all what we have discussed in the book so far and ask yourself if you are ready to learn, so that you are protecting yourself when learning **How to win when deal-**

ing with builders.

Please put yourselves in the position of the characters we discuss throughout this book and ask yourself questions. I feel we are all a little like Billy Bone Idol at times. I asked Billy another question after reading the answers: "Billy, if I said to you that if I pointed you in a certain direction and told you to keep walking in a reasonable straight line you would eventually find a million pounds, what would you do? Would you start walking?"

He answered "No!" so I asked why. The reason he said "no" was because he believed someone else would have found it before him. Would you say he lacked faith, belief, motivation, hope? Well I don't know if there would be one answer to this question or a mixture of them all. Do **you** lack any of the above? Are there areas you could improve in?

Well, I decided to work with Billy Bone Idol for six months or so, on and off, and I found that he was able to turn his whole attitude around after a while. Once he was shown respect and given encouragement to improve, it made all the difference. He didn't like having to take brickwork down at times due to it not being correctly built, but after the initial frustrating period of re-building the work he was able to develop the required skills to become a useful apprentice bricklayer. Billy made lots of mistakes and had to put them right, but after a while he became competent in the work he was doing.

That is the story of our lives, isn't it? Talking about sto-

171

ries, here is one that I shall never forget; it was when Billy Bone Idol became a human Catherine Wheel[7]. Talk about turning his whole attitude around. This is an incident that happened when Billy didn't listen to me.

Like I said before, health and safety is such an important area within any building work, especially when dealing with people who are ignorant to their own safety, let alone any other person's safety. Whenever you go onto a building site you need to make sure you are following health and safety procedures, which are set out by the Health and Safety Policy that all employers and employees should be aware of. Just have a read of this:

The Occupational Health and Safety Act 2004 was passed to protect the health and safety of people at work. It tells us what employers and employees are supposed to do to prevent injury or illness at work. Legislation has given voice to workers who now have protection for their safety as part of an employer's duty of care. Occupational health and safety information plays a vital role in drawing attention to any problem or breach of regulation. An employee must ensure all staff are working in a safe and hazard free environment. What me and Bruiser do whenever anyone comes onto a job we are in charge of is, first, they must come to the office to sign the site book to say who they are and what firm they are presenting. All employees must have a site induction. They are told of the site proce-

---

7 A Catherine Wheel is a firework that revolves on a pin, making a wheel of fire or sparks.

dures in the event of a fire, reporting an accident, reporting a hazard, who the first aid representative is, and who the site foreman is, etc. Basically, it is a protection for themselves and everyone else on the job. The employer has a duty of care to the employees and the employees also have a duty of care to themselves and to all other people who are working on the job.

Billy Bone Idol received his site induction like everyone else and signed the form to say that this had taken place and that he understood it. Before he was allowed to use any equipment again he was informed what was expected and shown how to lift materials, etc. without endangering himself or others. Now the problem is that there are those in our industry who say that there is no need to wear the correct PPE (personal protective equipment) at times because they only get in the way.

An example would be when building a chimney. It would be fair to say that there is an unlikelihood of something falling from the sky, so would there be a need to wear a hard hat? I would agree under certain circumstances that it is not always necessary to wear certain clothing, but unfortunately, in my opinion, there is no such thing as common sense. As I've stated previously, people don't always see things the same way, so it is compulsory to wear PPE equipment at all times on certain work projects.

What I learnt where Billy Bone Idol was concerned is whether or not he can make an informed decision on what is safe or unsafe practice is very debateable. Just because Billy said he understood didn't mean that he

173

did. I guess there comes a time though when you only can do what you can do; that is by following the prescribed procedures that have been put in place.

A large cement mixer can be a dangerous piece of equipment, if not used correctly. This equipment has a drum that rotates and is used to mix sand, cement, and water together so that you have a mixture available called **mortar**. We use mortar to lay bricks on when building walls.

Billy Bone Idol was instructed not to place the head of the shovel in the mixer when he is placing the sand and cement in it as the mixer drum was rotating, because the shovel can get jammed in between the blades that are inside the mixer. It is so easy to be holding onto the shovel handle and easily break your wrist or arm if the shovel gets jammed. So what did our Billy do? You've got it, he did what he was told not to do and put the shovel head inside the mixer as it was rotating.

Well, before I could do anything, the handle of the shovel somehow got itself embedded in the front of Billy's jumper and because the mixer was going around Billy became the first human Catherine Wheel I've ever seen. He was being spun around in a complete circle. Now to see this was very funny, even though Billy didn't see it that way. It didn't help because he was so small and skinny, but it was a lesson for him. I remember telling him at the time; it could have been worse, it could have been me!

The thing is it could have been worse. That's what an

174

apprenticeship is all about: learning from your mistakes and learning to put them right. Avoidance is better than cure though, in most cases. Again this is what this book is all about, to show you how to avoid the possible hazards that will create pain if you are not careful. The beauty of this book is that you can secure the skills required to learn **How to win when dealing with builders** and avoid pain, if you listen and put yourself in the stories.

Bruiser was able to avoid Billy Bone Idol because when Bruiser was away at times I was able to have Billy with me on occasions. Bruiser still knew what was going on though, and I know he was finding it all very amusing.

It still amazes me when you see programmes on the TV like *Cowboy Builders*, when people just go against everything logical that says **don't do it**! I watched one programme where the builder said he wouldn't sign a contract prior to beginning the work. The reason he gave was that it is something he doesn't do, but the people still decided to have him do the job. Guess what? When they had problems with the builder, and he decided not to carry on doing the work, they found themselves with a big problem. They of course decided the builder was a cowboy builder. You know what, they were probably right. But who was at fault in the first place?

Look, I'm not saying that there are people out there who are not gullible or vulnerable, but it really frustrates and annoys me and Bruiser when this can be avoided with a little education and common sense.

175

OK, there is no such thing as common sense, some of you will be saying. To some extent I agree, due to how people view things. So please help us to begin educating the people you come into contact with now that you have the knowledge you are receiving.

Do we have a deal? Great! Once again this section is hopefully helping you to become more aware of how people think, the strange things people may do, and what you can learn from what you have read. I feel that the more we read something the more we can get out of it. As we grow by experiences, me and Bruiser have found that our views and our understandings change. That is why we recommend that the more you read this book the more you will get out of it. Please let us know how you get on.

Summary
- **Assessing competence**
- **Health and Safety**
- **Have the right attitude**
- **Learning terminology**
- **Ask questions**
- **Ask yourself 'What if?'**
- **Put yourself in the stories**
- **Following procedures**
- **Avoiding the mixer hazards**
- **Contracts are important**

SECTION 16:
The Dynamic Duo

"So Bruiser, what do we talk about so that we can share some more of our experiences with our friends?"

"Tell them about Dick Ward and his mate!"

"Dick Ward and his mate? What are you talking about now?"

"You know, Batman and Robin? The Dynamic Duo!"

I know what Bruiser is talking about. This was a TV programme back in the 60s and the actor who played Robin the boy wonder. The actor's real name was Burt Ward not Dick Ward. Bruiser used to call him Dick because of how he looked. The actor who played Batman was Adam West.

This was another of Bruiser's favourite TV programmes, but again the Gypsy Jim syndrome reared its ugly head with the name 'Dick' coming into Bruiser's mind. I find it quite funny though. But who are Batman and Robin, the Dynamic Duo, you may be asking yourself, in the real life situation?

We came across a couple of workmen years ago, who we called the Dynamic Duo, who seemed to have all the answers when it came to doing building work for people, but were never asked the right questions by

178

their customers. This was a typical cowboy operation, in our opinion.

They had all the talk and drove around in their very own Batmobile, as we called it. The vehicle was overloaded with tools and equipment, which looked good but they didn't know what to do with them. Don't be fooled by the equipment; it's how you use it that's important. (Where have I heard that before?) It's the same old problem arising when dealing with some builders. They give a lot of answers to people before starting the job, but people don't know the questions to ask them in the first place to get the right answers.

Just in case this doesn't make sense to you, I'll try and explain. Here is an example: Batman may say something like "Right, what we're going to do is strip the old plaster off that area of the wall and then replace the old plaster with some new plaster!" Now that may sound fine to begin with, but what happens when the Boy Wonder, Robin, spreads the plaster on the wall and after a couple of days the new plaster suddenly falls off the wall? Great, that's all you need.

Batman and Robin would have got into their Batmobile and driven to Gotham City to their Bat Cave with your money. (Thanks for allowing me to play, I like telling these types of stories as you've probably gathered by now). But if you could become an NVQ Assessor (NVQ stands for National Vocational Qualification) when dealing with builders, you would ask the questions to find out what they were going to do before putting the plaster on the wall. By doing this, you can

179

limit the possibility of it falling off once the plaster-work has been completed.

So what do I mean if you become an NVQ Assessor? What me and Bruiser want to share with you are some of our secrets and give you some basic principles we have learnt when it comes to working with other trades. As I've said previously, it will give you a great advantage when learning **How to win when dealing with builders** when you know what to say and what to ask them prior to the job starting and while the job is being done. This information will save you a lot of money and give you some amazing results, if you follow our procedure.

I told you in the creds section that I'm a qualified NVQ Assessor and Bruiser is also. Basically, what that means is that we are accredited to assess the competence of a person in relation to certain trades, so they can be deemed capable to have a recognised qualification in that trade. What Me and Bruiser want to share with you are some of the questions you need to ask builders so that you are covering the possibility of not having a nightmare situation happen to you. We want you to think as an NVQ Assessor would be thinking. So here are your NVQ assessment questions to ask.

Sound good? Great, let's begin.

The NVQ Assessment
Let us go over the basic questions we would be asking anyone who was employed to do a job, no matter what

180

trade they were going to perform.

The first question we ask is to determine competence. Don't forget, a piece of paper to say they are competent doesn't mean they are. Neither does giving the right answers, but it helps to have both. You will be the judge. So the question would be:

"What is the first thing you would do when you turn up on the job, prior to starting the work?" We would expect the answer to be "**to complete a risk assessment**".

A risk assessment is a careful examination of what could cause harm to people before the work activity commences and during the work activity. In a risk assessment you need to:

1. Look for the hazards.
2. Decide who might be harmed and how.
3. Evaluate the risks and decide whether the existing precautions are adequate or whether more should be done.
4. Record the findings where necessary.
5. Review the assessment.

Examples of what to consider include:

- Work activity.
- The equipment to be used.
- The duration of the work.
- The location of where the work activity is to take place and the presence of hazards such as an

181

open excavation, underground services, etc.

- The working environment, e.g. weather conditions and lighting.
- Condition and stability of existing work surfaces.
- Physical capabilities of the workers, e.g. pregnancy, vertigo sufferers.

Further advice on risk assessments can be obtained from HSE guidance: Five steps to risk assessment leaflet INDG 163(rev1) HSE books 1998 (I have taken the above risk assessment information from the HSE).

Make sure the contractor is aware of a site induction procedure and if not ask yourself why.

Site safety induction
Now these procedures are basic procedures and all credible builders should know these.

The site induction is carried out on site prior to anyone working on the job. A site induction sheet is normally provided with the relevant information recorded and signed by the individual operatives, once the site induction procedure has been completed.

The site induction sheet is read and discussed by all persons employed on or visiting the operational site and confirmed on the sheet by signature.

What is on the sheet?
Management team: contracts manager, site manager, foreman/woman.

182

Project particulars: site address, site telephone number, location and limits of use, site layout, access, egress, boundaries, etc.

Welfare facilities: canteen, toilets, drying room, storage container.

Procedure requirements

Reporting accidents, first aid, first aid facilities, fire precautions, evacuation, non-smoking, PPE requirements, scaffolds, housekeeping (removing rubbish, etc.), storage of materials, record of training, consultation (if you had any concerns regarding health and safety, etc.), common arrangements (shared welfare for all subcontractors, scaffolding by agreement, parking of vehicles etc.), site rules, site induction log (all operatives and visitors who have attended the induction are to sign the induction log), open discussion (an opportunity at the end of the induction for questions and discussions).

Once the induction has been completed, a declaration is signed. The wording would be something like this:

I *the undersigned have been inducted on health and safety for the above project and understand my duties and responsibilities on the project. I also acknowledge that failure to comply with the foregoing procedures may result in disciplinary procedure.*

This is dated, operative name printed and signed, company name, and signature of the site manager.

Evacuation procedure

An evacuation procedure is also signed. This would be in the form of something like this:

In the event of a fire or dangerous occurrence the person who discovers the same should raise the alarm at one of the designated fire control points located at various positions within the development and arrange for company staff to be informed immediately. All persons evacuating the site <u>must</u> report to the designated <u>assembly point</u>, which on this project is situated:

Signature ....

All operatives should report to this area to enable an appropriate head count to be taken. On no account should any one re-enter the building without prior consent of the person in charge.

The information above was taken from an actual site form me and Bruiser had to sign once.

A good website for guidance is www.hse.gov.uk for all health and safety information. HSE is an abbreviation of Health and Safety Executive: they provide free booklet guides, etc. in relation to health and safety. We've gone over this information with you because it is so important when dealing with builders that you are aware of correct procedures. If the builder isn't aware, does that mean they are going to be thinking about your welfare? You will have to ask yourself that question.

Me and Bruiser want to get rid of cowboy builders as much as you do. The only way we are going to achieve

184

this is through education. If you educate yourself you can educate someone else, then eventually there will be no more **cowboy builders**. OK, I can dream, can't I? Unfortunately there will no doubt be people who shall continue to get ripped off, but you are not going to be one of them, are you?

Please say you're not going to be one of them.

Summary
- **Ask the right questions**
- **Don't be fooled by their equipment**
- **Become an NVQ Assessor**
- **Risk assessments**
- **Site safety procedures**

How to win when dealing with builders

SECTION 17:
Trade talk

OK, what we want to go over with you now is some trade information for you to be aware of. We will go over the tools, equipment, and how the work is completed from start to finish. We will review what a trade's person would say and do in relation to **Plasterwork/Ceramic Tiling/Painting**. The reason for this is so that you will know what questions to ask and how the job should be completed. This will be a guarantee for you so that you will save money and protect yourself. Trust me and Bruiser on this; and read these procedures for your protection. The basic risk assessment procedure at the beginning of any job would be answered in the same way as stated in the NVQ Assessor section, so use this as the basis for the three trades we will be discussing in this section. The three trades I've listed are the basic trades you would come across in any maintenance work.

Plasterwork

If I was asking the candidate a question in relation to the tools and equipment required for a plastering operation, the response could be in this manner.

The Plaster Hawk is one of many plasterers' tools. A hawk consists of a board of about 25cm (9 inches) square together with a handle fixed centrally on the reverse. The purpose of a hawk is to hold the prepared

187

plaster ready for application. A plasterer would hold the hawk horizontally in his secondary hand whilst using a plaster trowel in his other hand to apply the wet plaster to the working surface. Hawks can also be used by bricklayers or brick pointers to hold mortar in the same way.

Plaster Bucket

One of the simplest yet essential plasterer's tools is a bucket in which to mix the plaster. A large flexible bucket is best as these are easy to clean by bending the bucket to break off the dried on plaster.

The float

A float is usually manufactured out of polycarbonate and is normally used when rendering a wall. Plasterer's trowels are sometimes referred to as floats, but strictly speaking a trowel is made from metal whilst a float is made from polycarbonate or another similar material.

Plasterers Brushes/Splash Brush

The splash brush, as the name suggests, is used to splash the wall with water between the second and third stage of the plastering process, just in advance of the final smoothing. Brushes may also be used to clean other equipment once the job is complete.

Mixing Paddle/stick

A mixing paddle or mixing stick of around 2 foot (Approx. 61cm) length can be used to mix the plaster ready for application in place of a powered mixer. A manual paddle would be used where only a limited amount of plaster is required, when doing home DIY for example.

188

Plaster mix

This is not a plasterer's tool but choosing the right plaster mix is important. It is available in various brands and types, gypsum-based plaster and cement-based plaster. Gypsum-based plaster is a porous plaster that is usually used indoors, as it will crumble and deteriorate if it becomes wet. Gypsum-based plaster can be purchased in a variety of forms, but browning, bonding, and metal lathing plaster are the most common. Cement-based plaster has a very different consistency from gypsum-based plaster meaning that it will not deteriorate as easily.

So let's go over the plastering operation as if spoken by the candidate (plasterer).

Candidate speaking:

I would first make sure that the background surface is free from any debris such as grease and any loose plaster, etc. Using the correct tools and equipment in the form of a scraper to remove any loose debris, sugar soap to remove any grease, and a hammer and bolster in the case of larger debris to be removed. The use of the correct PPE is used in the form of eye goggles, gloves, and overalls, if required.

Once the background surface has been prepared I would prepare the browning plaster, by the use of a bucket of water and would sprinkle in the plaster whilst mixing to form a smooth consistency. Once the plaster has been mixed, I would scoop enough plaster onto my plaster trowel and proceed to spread the plaster onto the wall, leaving around 10mm below the finished sur-

189

face ready to apply the finish plaster once the browning had set sufficiently. Once the browning plaster was set enough, ready to take the finish plaster, I would mix the finish plaster in the same way as the browning plaster and apply the finish plaster in one circular action with the plaster trowel. I would then apply enough water as required, with the use of the wet brush to the finish plaster, so that the plaster would be finished to a smooth glossy texture ready for painting.

Once the plastering operation has been completed the tools used for plastering can be cleaned by use of the bucket of water. Any waste material is collected and disposed of either in a waste bag or in the general skip if the job is big enough. In the case of any asbestos found during the assessment period this would have to be removed by a specialist company under HSE guidelines.

End of response.

The above answers by the candidate would be deemed a competent explanation by me and Bruiser.

Candidate questioning prior to plastering application

OK, I'm going to go over the questions me and Bruiser would ask when first dealing with candidates in relation to NVQ questioning, when applying the plaster to a wall. Think about you asking these questions to prospective builders.

190

Questions 1-7

1. So, give me some information about you. How long have you been working as a plasterer and who have you worked for?

2. What qualifications do you have? Where can the evidence be found?

3. When you start a job what is the first thing you do? (Risk assessment)

4. What PPE equipment do you carry with you?

5. What tools and equipment will you be using for the job?

6. Just talk me through the plastering procedure from start to finish.

7. What do you do after the job is completed?

What we want to do now is go through what we expect the person to say. We didn't say that learning **How to win when dealing with builders** was going to be easy, but if you get this right you are going to be in the winning position.

Think of this book as an elephant. If me and Bruiser asked you to eat an elephant what would you do? Would you eat it all at once or a piece at a time? OK, you wouldn't want to eat an elephant, but if you were hungry enough what would you do? Bruiser would probably be able to eat the elephant all at once, but for us mere mortals we would have to eat it **a piece at a time**. Agreed? Great!

That is what it's all about. You will all be at different levels when learning **How to win when dealing**

with builders, so take from this book what you need, whenever you need it. With the rest of the information, keep it stored away to use at a later date or to educate someone else with. Actually, better still, go and tell someone else to buy this book!

Answers to questions 1-7

1. When you ask your builder about himself you want to know what he has done before, so that you can check it out. Just because someone gives you an impressive CV, don't take their word for it. **Go and check the references out. This is very important**.

   You go and check the job references because you want to check the quality of work they have done. Again, don't just phone up to get a reference; they might have you call their best mate who is in on **ripping you off**.

2. Like I said before, when it comes down to qualifications what do they really mean? Does it make the person a good tradesman? Does it mean he knows what he is doing? Does it mean he's creditable? Well, the answer to these questions should be yes, but unfortunately life in the building game isn't as simple as that most of the time. We are not saying that it's not good to have the piece of paper as a qualification because it is, especially if the builder is credible as well. But never judge the book by its cover.

   Me and Bruiser have enjoyed helping builders

192

who have been in the building game for years, so they are able to get their piece of paper (qualification that is), because they have earnt a living for years and deserve the extra credibility. This may sound like a contradiction when I say they don't need a piece of paper to say they are competent. In reality, it's all about what the work looks like and what they have done to achieve the finished product. Certain trades require the piece of paper, such as electricians and plumbers dealing with gas appliances, so check out the requirements in the Building work requirements section.

3. Why is it important to ask this question?

If you remember, earlier in the book I told you about when I was a foreman for a while for a subcontractor. I remember seeing the bricklayers get out of their cars and I knew straight away that they weren't experienced bricklayers. Why? Because they didn't go to where most experienced bricklayers went, as soon as they arrived on site, in my experience. Where is that you may ask? To the canteen! Nine times out of ten, it's just the way it is. Most trades go to the canteen first, so they can get their food sorted out and know where they are going to be sitting come break time. This wasn't the only reason I knew they were not experienced, but it was the first alarm bell for me. The reason for asking question number 3 is because, again, as an assessor there is a process I'd want to hear from the candidate. (Don't forget you too

193

are an assessor to confirm competence).

I know I have risk assessment next to the question in number 3, which is very important. I would expect the contractor to say that they would be assessing the area of work for health and safety work hazards. This is something I would advise you to get fixed in your mind. The above observation I gave you when I was a foreman is one of the things you instinctively know due to experience and I'm aware that you are not necessarily in that situation. Over time you too would know just by looking at someone if they are competent or not, but initially just follow the steps we have given you. Look, they may turn up and just put their tools and materials down and that's it, they may be very competent, but if I were you I'd do what we are suggesting you should do. It gives you credibility!

Perception is what it's all about!

You don't have to be an expert, but if you look like you know what you are talking about you are going to come out smelling of roses. Again just because tradesmen/women come in and not do a risk assessment, this doesn't necessarily mean they are cowboys: it just means they may need educating to do this. When you do a job day in day out, you know yourself, it becomes routine, so we don't bother to do certain things after a while. In the building game, if we get complacent this is when there is likely to be an accident. The main cause of injuries is the dreaded **slips and trips**, as I've stated before.

4. They need to be carrying or have access to PPE. Don't allow any builder on your job unless they have this. They all should carry the basics as we've discussed: hard hat, eye goggles, dust masks, safety boots, overalls, gloves, ear defenders, first aid kit, etc. Again the HSE (Health and Safety Executive) have free information for builders and for you to know what is required, so there is no excuse.

    Don't take risks with your wellbeing!

    Don't forget we all have a duty of care for each other. Don't expect the builder to be thinking of your wellbeing, because they may not care. Are you in shock with that statement? Never mind if you are, please just get over it. Me and Bruiser want you to be safe.

5. Now this is where you can impress. Once you get into conversation with the plasterer, you can begin dropping some subtle questions, for instance about what type of float they use, what type of hawk they use, etc. Once again it comes back to **perception** (it's all a game). By the time we are finished, you will have enough information to be able to fool me and Bruiser when it comes down to credibility. Make sure we don't see our book lying about though. Actually I wouldn't worry if the book was lying about, because they may be

195

thinking you have been doing your homework in relation to what is required. You will probably know more than most of the builders anyway by the time you have finished this book. I jest not.

I shall talk through what I would be expecting to hear.

6. Here is a possible candidate response:

Before I begin the plastering activity, I would check that the wall surface to be plastered was free from any debris, such as old loose plaster that requires removing, and make sure the working surface is free from dust and grease. Once I've assessed the wall area to be plastered, if I needed to remove any old plaster I would wear my PPE such as eye protective goggles, gloves, overalls, etc.

I would use my hammer and bolster to remove the old plaster from the wall and then make sure the background surface is free from dust. The reason for this is so that the new plaster would be able to adhere to the wall. Any holes to be filled would be by use of suitable filler, and then allowed to dry.

I may use a suitable bonding agent to apply to the wall so that the plaster will adhere to the wall even better. Once the background surface has been prepared I would then be mixing my undercoat plaster known as **browning**. I would be using a plastic bucket with a suitable amount of water in it, then sprinkle the plaster into the bucket of water whilst mixing the water and plaster together. Once the plaster and water have mixed to a smooth consistency, and after dampening my hawk prior to putting an amount of plaster onto it, I am then ready to plaster.

Getting the plaster table ready and placing the mixed plaster onto it, I am now ready to apply a heap of plaster onto the hawk ready to spread onto the wall with my float. Dampening the float is important so that the plaster doesn't stick to it, so that once an amount of plaster has been scooped from the hawk onto the float it is easy to spread onto the wall area about 10mm (Approx.2/5 inch) thick. Once the wall has been plastered, a **browning rod** or straight edge is run across the surface to ensure there are no holes in the plaster surface and the wall is smooth from top to bottom.

Although the sand in the mixture theoretically provides enough texture for the finish coat to bond with, a cement brush may be dragged across the surface to slightly roughen it and help hold the finish coat. After allowing the browning coat to dry thoroughly, the **final coat or finish coat is** applied. This final coat is trowel led onto the **browning coat** in smooth arcs with the trowel never leaving the wall to eliminate trowel marks. Once the plaster begins to dry out it is **water trowel led** (this means sprayed with small

197

amounts of water and trowel led to a smooth finish). Once the plaster on the wall has been allowed to dry out thoroughly, it is ready to be primed and painted.

This is the end of the example.

Hopefully this has given you a much better understanding of how a plastering operation should be done. This is essentially a plastering operation explanation that has been given to me as an Assessor. After watching the candidate put into practice what they have explained, I have deemed the candidate competent. Ultimately, this is all you want to require; that is, a competent job being completed. Again there is no such thing as a perfect job, in my opinion, because it's so easy to pick fault with anything.

7. Once the job is completed, all tools and equipment are washed and cleaned.

Now for the next trade.

Ceramic Tiling

Ceramic tiles provide a decorative feature to a wall and are long lasting. The tiles are easy to take care of and are almost impossible to mark or stain. Wall tiles can be installed literally any place where you want to be able to enjoy their pleasing feature, but the obvious locations are in the kitchen (as backsplashes or countertops) and in bathrooms and showers. Most people

198

think ceramic tiles are difficult to install, but the reality is it's not beyond the range of any handy DIY person who is willing to spend some time understanding the process and take their time installing the tiles to the wall. Ceramic tiles are available in lots of sizes from 25 square millimetres and usually sold attached to sheets that are 25x25mm all the way up to around 460mm approximately.

Me and Bruiser don't like metric measurement, we like imperial measurement. So it would be one square inch and sold attached to sheets that are twelve inches by twelve inches all the way up to eighteen inches. There you go; you've got the best of both. They also come in a wide range of colours that can tie with any decor. Actually all ceramic tiles don't resist water. (We bet you didn't know that).

The fact is some ceramic tiles, called non-vitreous, will actually absorb water, so they should only be used in areas where they won't come in contact with water. Semi-vitreous and impervious ceramic tiles both resist water (impervious tiles won't absorb any water at all).

If you are looking to put tiles on a bathroom or kitchen wall, make sure the tiler uses semi-vitreous or impervious tiles.

Now preparing the background surface prior to tiling would be the same procedure as plastering, with the same PPE. So please go and look back over the procedure again.

199

Once the candidate has gone over the preparation stage, we then ask for an explanation as to what is the next procedure in laying the tiles from start to finish.

A typical response from the candidate would be as follows:

After preparing the background surface I would then measure the area to be tiled with my tape measure by measuring the height x the width to receive the area square metre. Once this has been done, I would be able to determine how many tiles I would need. Once I have determined the amount of tiles I would need, I would then set out the tiles dry before applying any adhesive to the wall. I would do this by finding the centre of the wall by using my tape measure and pencil. Once the centre was determined I would scribe a vertical and horizontal line down and across the centre point of the wall to act as a guide for the dry tiles to be laid from. This is done to form the pattern as to where the tiles would be applied by moving the tiles out from the centre to the sides horizontally; this would determine where any cuts would be needed at the sides.

The next step would be to apply the tile adhesive onto the wall with the help of the notched trowel and fix the tiles onto the adhesive. I would make sure I leave spaces between the tiles with the aid of the spacers. In order to attach the tiles firmly to the adhesive, I would twist the tile a little on the adhesive to cause a firm fit. The tiles would be laid horizontally and at a row at a time on top of one another. Once I had dry laid the tiles out towards the side edges, any cuts that I would need to do would be done using the tile snips. If the tiles are

200

sharp at the edges after snipping has been completed, I would use the sandpaper to smooth these edges. I would leave the tiles overnight to dry and bond properly with the adhesive for the whole night period.

Once I had ensured the tiles had dried the next day and I had removed the tile spacers, the next step would be to grout the tiles. The grout is applied to seal the gaps between the tiles and acts as a water preventative and gives a decorative feature. I would be applying the grout at an approximate 45 degree angle with the help of the rubber float.

Any excess or unwanted grout mix can be removed by the damp sponge. After around 60-70 minutes, the haze that appears on the tiles from the use of the grout and sponge can be buffed up with the aid of a dry rag. The final procedure would be to use the caulk, which acts as a sealant around the edges of the tile.

Once the tiling operation has been completed the tools used for tiling can be cleaned by use of the bucket of water. Any waste material is collected and disposed of either in a waste bag or in the general skip if the job is big enough. In the case of any asbestos being found during the assessment period, this would have to be removed by a specialist company under HSE guidelines.

End of response.

Painting

Again, the preparation of the background surface and the risk assessment procedure is exactly the same as the Plastering and Tiling operations. Therefore, the candidate response would be as previously given.

The candidate would be asked to give a list of the tools and equipment needed. The response would be as follows.

Candidate speaking:

I would have a list of tools and equipment in the form of:

1. **A decorator's brush**

   A decorating brush will generally have longer bristles to hold more paint, which creates less spillage and gives a smoother result.

2. **Spray gun**

   The spray gun is ideal for small to medium painting projects around the house such as fences, decking, etc. The spray gun can cope with thin to medium materials such as semi-transparent stain, clear wood preservative, water sealer, varnish, oil-based paint or stain.

3. **Paint brush**

   There is a large range of paint brushes available on the market so it is best to choose the ones suitable for the job to be done.

4. **Paint kettle**

   A paint kettle is used to store unused paint to prevent it drying out or to clean the dirty brushes in.

5. **Paint pads**

Paint pads are used for painting large areas of smooth walls to give a better finish without leaving brush strokes.

6. **Paint roller**

Using a paint roller to apply the paint will save time and produce a more uniformed finish. If the wall is not smooth then a softer roller with a longer pile can be used.

7. **Extension poles for paint rollers**

Paint roller extension poles are great for reaching higher parts of walls without the need to use a ladder. This makes extension poles ideal for painting ceilings of rooms.

8. **Replacement paint roller heads**

Replacement roller heads are ideal for painting and decorating. Roller heads are good replacements and are very useful for covering large areas of the wall in short spaces of time.

9. **Paint scrapers for painting and decorating**

Paint scrapers are ideal for scraping old paint off the walls and other surfaces before repainting them afterwards. It also allows for an even surface to paint over.

10. **Paint trays for painting**

Paint trays are ideal for holding paint, and come in various sizes for rollers and paint brushes.

11. **Painter's putty**

Painter's putty is a water base compound that is used to face glaze wood and metal sash. It is used to fill countersunk nail heads, crevices, and cracks. It is specifically designed for use under all types of water base paint (interior and exterior). It is equally effective under conventional oil base paints.

12. **Caulk**

Decorator's caulk is a white emulsion-based sealant and filler used for repairing cracks and gaps around skirting boards, architrave, door frames, and windows.

End of response.

By now you should be getting a feel for what you would be expecting to hear from a tradesman.

Let's go over the candidate response in completing a Painting job. Let's say a bedroom that needs to be painted.

Candidate speaking:

Painting Woodwork and Walls

Once I've determined what tools and equipment I'm going to need for the job, I then sort out the materials required. In the case of painting, the room would need to be cleared of unnecessary furniture or the furniture would need to be covered with a suitable form of sheeting. The preparation of the woodwork for painting is basic work. I would remove the hardware such as knobs, handles, and locks. It is easier to take them off than to try to paint around them and achieve neat results.

204

If the surface is dirty or greasy I would clean it and allow it to completely dry. Sugar soap is a very good cleaning substance to use. I would also be looking at filling any nail holes with wood or painter's putty. Wood putty would need to be sanded when dry and then primed. Any bare surface should be primed. This would include any new wood or a surface that has been scraped or sanded down to the bare surface. A sealing primer will prevent the finish coat from being absorbed, ensuring an even gloss or sheen finish.

I would prime new wood and then allow it to dry. After I had completed this task I would then use caulk to fill any cracks. The reason for using caulk is because it adheres better to a primed or painted surface.

(Smart candidate this one, you always get them.)

I would then sand all surfaces to ensure good adhesion of the new paint to the old paint and achieve a smooth finish. It's important to vacuum and wipe down the surface with a damp cloth to remove any dust. Whether I use alkyd (commonly known as oil based paint) or acrylic paint, thinning may be helpful to achieve a smooth, level finish. Not only can thinning improve the look of the finish, but this can also ease the painting application. The problem is some paint is too thick to flow smoothly out of the brush when I'm painting. When I add a little thinner to the paint, it really helps the paint to flow better onto the surface. I use the appropriate thinner or mineral spirit for alkyd paint and water for acrylic paint.

When painting an interior wall I would make sure the wall surface was free from grease or loose paint by using sugar soap and a paint scraper respectively. Any holes that were available would be filled using suitable filler. Once this was done I would make sure before painting that it was sanded down and any dust removed. I would use a matt finish or gloss finish emulsion paint and would choose the correct tools and equipment to accomplish the painting task. I would use a suitable sized cutting in brush to paint around the edges of the wall before using a paint roller or paint pad to apply the first coat of paint. A second coat of paint would be applied once the first coat has dried sufficiently. If the ceiling needed to be painted I would do exactly the same procedure as I've stated with the painting of a wall.

Cleaning the tools and equipment is done after the painting task is completed. If oil based paint is used I would use white spirit to remove the paint from the brush head. If water based paint was used I would use water to clean the tools and equipment.

End of response.

We have gone over some examples of what tools and equipment can be used for the three trades, as well as what type of response me and Bruiser would expect

206

from a candidate who we were assessing. This is just one way of assessing competence. Is this the only way? No!

Some may say this is not how they would do the operation; we would do this or do that. Me and Bruiser would say, "Great, so do that then!" All we are trying to show you is a method of becoming confident when learning **How to win when dealing with builders**.

We suggest you learn something about the tools, equipment, and the job that you want doing, so that you are **less likely to get ripped off**. Yes, we know you should be able to trust someone to come into your world and help you to live happily ever after, but life is not always as easy as that. We are showing you one way of **How to win when dealing with builders**, but it doesn't mean you have to do what we suggest. Ultimately, it is entirely up to you.

We hope this has been useful. We need your feedback, so we know what you would like us to do in the future to help you. By the way, keep your suggestions clean please: me and Bruiser are very sensitive souls really.

Summary

- **Plasterwork**
  - **Tools and equipment**
  - **Application procedure questioning**
- **Ceramic Tiling**
  - **Tools and equipment**
  - **Application procedure questioning**
- **Painting**
  - **Tools and equipment**
  - **Application procedure questioning**
- **Learn the language**

SECTION 18:
The Smooth Operator and Eddie the Elevator

Me and Bruiser have been having a chat about any way we can help you in relation to keeping your contract with your builder in check. Bruiser came up with the names Dicky Eddie and the Smooth Operator. Actually what he meant was Tricky Eddie. So who is Tricky Eddie, whose nickname was changed to Eddie the Elevator after so many people in the building game had dealings with him? He was someone to look out for, so you didn't get any surprises.

You all have had experiences in shopping centres where you go up and down on elevators, haven't you? Well, Eddie the Elevator could be classed as a human elevator who always went up in price. And then we have The Smooth Operator. Well, this is his story.

Many years ago, I came across a ground worker who we nicknamed The Smooth Operator. Why? This was because he had learnt the hard way when he first had dealings with a main contractor. What he shared with me and Bruiser has held us both in good stead ever since, when dealing with building contractors. He was offered a contract to take on a major ground working project and thought he had won the pools. (In those days it was Littlewoods' Pools that could make you a millionaire). What happened then was that as soon as The Smooth Operator had started a contract, the main

210

contractor offered him more and more contracts until he had become the main ground work contractor for the company.

Now, The Smooth Operator had to deal with a lot of financial outlay, with materials and labour costs, due to the amount of work he had taken on. He said that the first 12 months was great; he was getting well paid for the work he was doing. Then all of a sudden there were problems with payments from the main contractor. Why? Because the main contractor was finding reasons why they shouldn't pay for all of the work he was doing. The retention money is money that is held back until the other party's work has been deemed to be completed to the agreed contract specifications. In other words, they were holding him to ransom.

The Smooth Operator said it became a nightmare for him. In a short period he was in debt due to not getting all the money he should have been paid, which was due to the overhead payments he was obliged to pay. Holding back retention money is a ploy some companies use to get money from you with no intention of paying you back. As I've stated before, the easiest thing in the world is to find fault with someone's workmanship. The Smooth Operator told me that once he was free from the contracts he had taken on, he would never put himself in that position again.

Due to his bad experiences, he informed me that when he finished any stage operation he would send his invoice in for payment. This would include added extras for unforeseen work that would have been required to

211

complete. He stated at the beginning of any job that there was always unforeseen work that would be required to complete, which wasn't part of the contract agreement. He made sure there was a clause within the contract that stipulated that if any unforeseen extra work was required, an addition payment would be needed to be paid by the contractor.

Make sure you are aware of any extra payment clauses within contracts you deal with, so there are no surprises.

On every job The Smooth Operator starts now, he always makes sure there are extra payments that he submits in his first invoice. He knows by experience that at the end of the contract most firms will always come up with some problems they have found so that they don't pay for all of the work completed. This is a way they make money out of people; as I've stated before, it's all a game.

So who is Eddie the Elevator?

Well, Eddie the Elevator worked as a quantity surveyor for the contract company The Smooth Operator worked for. A quantity surveyor manages all costs relating to building and civil engineering projects, from the initial calculations to the final figures. Now surveyors should be seeking to minimise the costs of a project and enhance value for money, while still achieving the required standards and quality.

212

Wow, you might be thinking, Eddie the Elevator is a nice man. Well, depending on what side of the fence you are on, you may be right. And, yes, there are some nice Eddie the Elevators out there who would be classed as good ethical people. What you need to be aware of though is there may be an Eddie the Elevator working for your builder who is not one of the nice people and will be giving him some money-saving advice at your expense. So expect your initial price to be elevated before the work is completed, that way you are not going to have a surprise.

That is where you can become The Smooth Operator. I can hear my One in a Trillion (my wife) now saying, "I wish you would be more trusting like me!" My answer to her would be, "Yes, Gorgeous, and one day Bruiser will become a brain surgeon." I've been in the building game long enough now not to trust myself in certain situations, let alone someone else. That's why I don't put myself into certain situations, so I'm not going to trust other people. (Bruiser's eyes are misting over right now; I think that was a little too deep for him).

Me and Bruiser recommend that you put a clause in the contract that states that if the work is not completed on time, there will be a penalty payment incurred. This could be on a sliding scale. As I have stated before, you need to be thinking outside of the box; you take control of the situation you are putting yourself in. You can also have an incentive clause put into the contract that says that if the work is completed before or on the agreed date, there would be a bonus payment given.

213

Some builders will definitely try and increase the initial agreement payment if they are able to. Their mate Eddie the Escalator will have thought of ways to apply that. I know that there are builders out there who will actually give you money back if they feel the work wasn't as expensive as they originally thought. You see, there are some good honest builders out there, like me and Bruiser. Again, **having an estimated quote is different from having a quote**. Remember that an estimated quote is a guess on the price given and an actual quote is a fixed price on a price given. Don't get the two mixed up.

Sound good? Great! Just learn the game rules, and you will be fine.

Summary
- **Elevated prices**
- **Retention payments**
- **Allow for unforeseen costs**
- **Have a clause in contracts for penalty or bonus payment**
- **Estimated quotes and actual quotes are different**
- **Learn the rules**

SECTION 19:
One of those everyday miracles

This was one of those times when I was with my One in a Trillion (remember, my wife). We were going to view an area where we were thinking of purchasing a property. It was the end of the working day and my wife and I decided to go and view the property just after the traffic rush period was over.

When we got to the area we began talking to a mother and daughter in relation to our business; I asked the mother if I could quickly go to my van and get a business card for her. She agreed and off I went. I opened the sliding door to my van, found my wallet, and after removing a card, I quickly slid the door shut. At that moment, it was as though time had stood still and an avalanche of thoughts rushed through my mind, all at once. I felt a cold chill pass through my body and, as I looked down, I saw the first finger of my left hand trapped in an 8mm (Approx. 1/3 inch) gap.

How can this be?

What have I done?

I can't have!

That's impossible!

Oh, no!

216

These are some of the many thoughts that raced through my mind. How can my finger be in such a tiny gap? I'd completely closed the door. I know this because I can see it; I heard the door slam shut. Is this really happening?

All of a sudden the pain associated with this event finally kicked in and I knew I'd made a big mistake. Again, thoughts came to the forefront of my mind. Have I lost part of my finger? It was as if I'd been there for hours, but it all took place within seconds.

I finally opened the door not knowing what to expect. I could see I had to get to hospital as soon as possible. I wrapped my handkerchief tightly around my finger, went over to my wife, and said, "We must go to the hospital now!"

When we arrived at the hospital we were asked to stay in the waiting room to see a doctor; this could take up to four hours. After the initial assessment by the nurse, it was concluded that the deep cuts I had on both sides of my finger needed to be treated. Miraculously there seemed to be no breaks. Well, at least one thing was real; it did take four hours before we finally saw a medic who attended my finger. Nightmare!

As I reflect on this time in my life I've learnt so much more about the everyday miracles that can be found through our adversities.

217

Miracle 1

I know my finger was trapped within an 8mm (Approx. 1/3 inch) gap because I measured the gap when the door of the van is shut. I also measured the side of my finger, which is 20mm   (Approx. just over ¾ inch) wide. How didn't I lose part of my finger?

How wasn't it at least broken?

Miracle 2

As I was waiting for treatment, I knew I was going to need stitches. Two fingers from my injured finger, I have another scar, on my little finger. This was the result of an accident where a stitch was administered by use of a needle some 40 years ago. I remember the event clearly and the pain associated with it. Now I had received a miracle of today's technology called **skin glue**, with no needles and hardly any pain when applied. What a miracle! I don't know why I didn't lose part of my finger or break it. I guess only God knows the reason why.

My wife is a constant shining example to me, as we walk the path of life together; she always sees the flowers that can be found amongst the weeds. Remember that the sun is always shining behind those dark clouds. Look beyond the scars and you can find the miracles associated with them, is mine and Bruiser's testimony.

Miracles do happen.

You are a miracle yourself, we all are. In all that you do, just **think eternal**! Me and Bruiser want to thank you for spending your valuable time with us in reading this book; to us that is a miracle. As we have stated before, it is a book for you and for everyone else who deserves to be treated differently when learning **How to win when dealing with builders**.

Our hope is that from this day forward whenever you need to deal with builders, or with people generally for that matter, you may want to refer back to this book and go over the stories and advice that we have given you. It was intended to just be a book on **How to win when dealing with builders** when we started out, but we now feel it has become more than that.

Writing this book has definitely changed my life for the better. I have been able to go back over some of the memories nobody can take away from me and Bruiser. We have been able to share part of our life stories I guess, when we have had to learn **How to win when dealing with builders**. It has been a great opportunity for me and Bruiser to reflect on some of the special people we've been able to associate with over the years. There have been some great characters that you have read about. We've been blessed to be able to share with you part of our building life journey.

Me and Bruiser would love to keep in touch with you and get to know you personally in the future. Please send your feedback to info@nabbab.com. We would love to be able to share more of our life experiences with you through further books and through our personal meetings with you. We have lots more funny stories and experiences to share, as I'm sure you have also. Be mindful of that. You are like no other person on earth; you are an individual put on the earth to fulfil your true potential and share with the rest of us what special gifts and talents you have.

Me and Bruiser believe that you do have special gifts and talents even though you may not be aware of them yet.

Typical, there is me pouring out my heart and soul to you, and my mate Bruiser Bruce is fast asleep, sucking his thumb, no doubt dreaming of more words of wisdom he wishes to share with you during our future meetings.

Thank you again for sharing your time with us and it's goodnight from Bruiser and life's best wishes from me.

Summary
- **Miracles do happen!**

Me and Bruiser's slang and phrase dictionary

Alarm Bells ringing	go by your feelings
A nicking was due	going to be arrested
Aggro	aggravation
A happy bunny	happy person
Booby prize	a prize for coming last
Bottle	courage
Bottled it	to lose courage
Builder's crack	describing the top of the buttocks
Chancers	to gamble on an outcome
Charge-hand	foreman or woman
Cheesing me off	getting annoyed
Charm job	made something sound good
Cracked up to be	sounding better than something is
Creds	credibility
Crud	rubbish; something useless
Dick	a contemptible person
Dickhead	stupid person
Dipstick	thick
Dopey prat	being a fool
Dropping you in it	getting into trouble

222

Dummy throwing	acting like a baby
Earache	incessant complaining or talking
Filling up	getting tearful
Get your head around	to understand
Going loopy	going mad or insane
Good vibes	good feelings
Gut feeling	what you feel deep inside
Head wen	got angry
Heave ho	to get rid of
Hump	to be in a bad mood
Joe Bloggs	average or unknown person
Keystone Kops	police
Load of bull	rubbish
Long arm of the law	police and the power of the law
Lowlife	contemptible and despised person
Mate	friend
Mickey	teasing
Muppet	idiot
Nicked	arrested
No brainer	obvious; don't have to think about something
PC	police constable
Power trip	using a person's given authority excessively

Prized Assets	ask Bruiser ☺
Pub	public house
Punter	customer
Rid	discard
Ripped off	con or swindle
Run in	confrontation
Sack them	to dismiss
Shady	suspicious in nature; dodgy; sketchy
Soul brother	a fellow black male
Smelling of roses	smelling nice
Stitch-up	to betray
Take the Mickey	to tease; to ridicule
The once ove	to check something
Verbal	talking
Winding up	being annoying
Work's do	party; get together
Working on the tools	physically working with tools; tradesperson